RABBIT HUNTING

SECRETS OF A MASTER COTTONTAIL HUNTER

OUTDOORSMAN'S EDGE®
GUIDES

RABBIT HUNTING

SECRETS OF A MASTER COTTONTAIL HUNTER

Dave Fisher

CRE▲TIVE
OUTDOORS™

Trade paperback edition frist published in 2004 by

CRE&TIVE
O U T D O O R S™

An imprint of Creative Homeowner®, Upper Saddle River, N.J.
Creative Homeowner® is a registered trademark of Federal Marketing Corporation.

Front Cover Photo: Don Jones
Back Cover Photos: David Fisher, Mitch Kezar/Windigo Images
Cover Design: Design Source Creative Services
Inside Images by David Fisher unless otherwise indicated
Photos by Ted Rose on pages 5, 10, 106, 112, and 142.
Illustrations by Andrew Keener

Printed in the United States of America
Current printing (last digit) 10 9 8 7 6 5 4 3 2 1
Library of Congress card number: 2004106456
ISBN: 1-58011-205-6

CREATIVE HOMEOWNER®
24 Park Way
Upper Saddle River, NJ 07458

TABLE OF CONTENTS

INTRODUCTION..vii

CHAPTER 1:   THE COTTONTAIL: A SPLIT PERSONALITY..........................1

CHAPTER 2:   HUNTING AT AUNT MILDRED'S....................................7

CHAPTER 3:   BETTER FIELD CARE MAKES BETTER EATING.................13

CHAPTER 4:   THE ROOTS OF BEAGLING....................................19

CHAPTER 5:   MEMORIES OF OUR GREATEST CHASES........................27

CHAPTER 6:   HARD TACK CANDY..41

CHAPTER 7:   SELECTING A BEAGLE: MALE OR FEMALE?.....................49

CHAPTER 8:   BEAGLE TRAINING..51

CHAPTER 9:   BUILDING A HUNTING PACK....................................69

CHAPTER 10: IN DAYS GONE BY..73

CHAPTER 11: SEEKING THE QUARRY..79

CHAPTER 12: WHY THEY CIRCLE AND WHY THEY HOLE UP.................85

CHAPTER 13: THE KENNEL..95

CHAPTER 14: MAKING SENSE OUT OF SCENTS...............................107

CHAPTER 15: CARING FOR YOUR BEAGLE.....................................113

CHAPTER 16: BREEDING YOUR BEAGLE.......................................131

CHAPTER 17: THE FIRST RABBIT VIDEOS....................................143

CHAPTER 18: THE MYSTERY IN LAUREL SWAMP.............................151

CHAPTER 19: THOSE SPECIAL MOMENTS......................................157

CHAPTER 20: SNOWSHOE HARE HUNTING....................................171

CHAPTER 21: THE GIFT...177

CHAPTER 22: RABBIT HUNTING'S FUTURE...................................185

EPILOGUE...193

INTRODUCTION

Why one settles on a specific sport, or a particular form of that sport, is anyone's guess. Somewhere along the line my sport became hunting. At first, it didn't matter what species I was hunting, so long as I was out in the woods or fields somewhere chasing something. Like many of us, I got started by hunting cottontails with the family dog. Cottontails were plentiful in those days, and Teddy, our dog (a mixed breed collie that never barked on trail), caught as many as I was ever able to take with gun. I've come a long way since then, but time, in some respects, has also stood still. While many of my friends have gone on to pursue much bigger game, and have become quite good at it, I continue to hunt cottontails.

Some will never understand my obsession with pursuing an animal that weighs less than five pounds, while I'm armed with a modern shotgun, and a pack of trailing hounds. But if you are reading this book, chances are that you already understand. Beagling is not just the pursuit, not just the kill. It is the whole experience of hound, cottontail, and hunter all combined into a medley only those who have heard and experienced can truly understand. To stand alone high on a stump and hear the hounds screaming at the top of their lungs; to see months and years of training culminate in a spectacular run, and finally see the rabbit coming full throttle straight for you; and to see him almost frozen in an instant of time as the shot connects and he tumbles into three inches of fresh snow; that is what rabbit hunting is all about. After hundreds, perhaps thousands, of times, I never get tired of it. I thank God I have been privileged to see it and be a part of it many, many times. Each chase seems new and different, and no matter how good I sometimes think I am, or how well my dogs work him over, Mr. Cottontail still manages to outsmart the dogs and me on many occasions. He and his many cousins are real survivalists, and they will be with us for a long time to come.

Since writing cottontail and hare articles for many of the outdoor magazines, two newspapers here in western Pennsylvania, and producing video tapes on hunting cottontails and hares, I subsequently get quite a few phone calls and letters from others interested in the sport. And I am amazed at the number of new hunters just getting into rabbit hunting and beagling. Some have never owned a dog before! This book is written mostly for them. Oh, I expect any beagle owner and rabbit chaser will enjoy it, as it will surely bring back memories and experiences that all of us have shared at one time or another.

First off, I would like to make it clear I do not consider myself an authority on the subject of rabbit hunting or the raising and training of gundogs. There are far more people better qualified to write or speak on the subject than I am. I do not specifically raise beagles to sell, and I could count on one hand the field trials I have attended. However, I am not a novice at the game, either. I am in my 50s, and have been chasing rabbits with dogs for more than 30 years. I have raised nearly 250 dogs, 100 for my own use, and have lost only a few due to illnesses. During an average Pennsylvania hunting season that is 10 weeks long, I will hunt at least seven solid weeks, then venture to a couple other states to extend my hunting.

I also do not intend this book to be a "how-to" manual on rabbit hunting, or on raising or training your particular dog. It is simply a collection of my thoughts, opinions, stories, and trial-and-error methods that have helped me consistently take cottontails, and develop some exceptional gundogs along the way. These are dogs that may never win a trophy at any trial or competition, but will get in the brush, roust a bunny, and bring him back to the gun: They are loyal hunters and companions in the field. In all my many years of hunting, I have had need for little else.

I also do not believe this book will ever become The Rabbit Hunter's Bible or anything like that. Due to time and space, or items that are simply beyond my field of expertise, some aspects of beagling will not be covered, but I hope to touch upon many of the things that have made the sport of rabbit hunting so special to me.

Finally, it should be noted that as a hunter gets more experienced, he will surely find himself at the stage where the kill is not as important as it once was. He may find himself intentionally letting a particularly crafty cottontail slip by after a fine chase. The hunter begins to value life a little more dearly. I find myself at this point in my life. I find myself wanting to leave something behind to let people know I was on the earth, and how I felt about the things I loved. Hunting cottontails is one of those things. It is my hope that one of these days, somewhere on a rabbit hunt, someone will mention my name and say, "Man, that guy sure loved to hunt rabbits!" And you can bet your best beagle . . . I will surely hear him.

THE COTTONTAIL: A SPLIT PERSONALITY

The house was only a couple hundred yards away when the dogs jumped the last rabbit of the day. In those days we gave little thought to waiting for the rabbit to circle or any such thing that would now be standard procedure. We just killed cottontails. So it wasn't unusual to stick to the dogs with youthful exuberance and shoot each cottontail as soon as they made a mistake.

This tenacious cottontail, however, would teach us something that has remained with me for the 34 years since that sunshiny fall afternoon. The rabbit was on a dead run for the house and garage and this was surely going to be a quick and easy kill. Behind the huge barn–type garage sat my older brother's '64 Ford Fairlane, which he had parked there before heading off to Vietnam. The car was still in driveable condition, and we used it to tear around the fields and play stock car.

The dogs pressed the cottontail under the Ford, and we again thought we would have this bunny in the pot in a few minutes. The dogs went in and out from under the car for 20 minutes and finally gave up. We investigated every hole in the frame, checked all the wheels, and we gave up too–the rabbit had disappeared.

The dogs were now at the house guzzling water and we decided that was a good idea. As we began to walk away, I looked back at the Fairlane one last time. Then it hit me! I walked over, popped the hood, and there was this big fat cottontail sitting smack dab on top of the air cleaner! He stared at me and I stared at him, and then with one leap he cleared the shiny red fender and really disappeared back into the brush. This was more than 30 years ago, but I remember it like it was yesterday!

From that point on I began to develop a legitimate admiration for the furry little creature with the cotton tail. I began to marvel at his tenacity for life, his ability to outmaneuver a pair of trailing hounds, and his inherent characteristic to circle back to his home turf. I no longer simply wanted to kill him, but now I enjoyed hunting him, trying to find out more about him, and just who exactly was this guy called Cottontail?

Mr. Cottontail is actually a creature with multiple personalities, depending on where he lives, and what type of predator is planning on having him for dinner. He is by far the most heavily pressured animal on earth.

Most of us hunt the cottontail, (1) *Sylvilagus floridanus*, probably the most abundant species in America. His main range is east of the Dakotas, down through Colorado, and into central Texas and on east to the Atlantic Ocean. His range also extends south and overlaps his southern cousin, *Sylvilagus palustrius*. That's right, the cottontail is not just one species but five separate varieties.

As mentioned, his next of kin is (2) *Sylvilagus palustrius*. Palustrius lives from eastern Virginia on south into Florida, and the Gulf States. Cane cutters and the blue-bellied swamp rabbits would more than likely fall into the palustrius variety. It would be safe to say that floridanus and palustrius commonly breed together, creating even more variations. Most southern hunters would be taking Sylvilagus palustrius.

Throughout the Rocky Mountains, the cottontail again changes his primary form to become (3) *Sylvilagus nuttalli*. With thick and heavy fur, the nuttalli is equipped to deal with the cold Rockies.

As the Rocky Mountains begin to sweep westward into the extreme western states the nuttalli is slowly replaced by the fourth species of cottontail, (4) *Sylvilagus auduboni*. Auduboni is found throughout the southwest into central and southern California. Don't confuse either of these species with jackrabbits or hares—they are not. They are simply a variety of cottontails. Jackrabbits and hares are a totally different species of rabbit and do not fall into the genus Sylvilagus.

The last cottontail is restricted to the Pacific Coast area of California, Washington, and Oregon. He is called (5) *Sylvilagus bachmani*, and makes up the smallest species of cottontail (in terms of numbers).

Even within the five species you may also have specific varieties, such as the New England woods rabbit, the Idaho desert bunny, or the large southern swamp rabbits with splayed and furred toes for swimming. It is thought that there may be as many as a dozen different kinds or types of cottontails. That's basically who Mr. Cottontail is, but there is a whole lot more about him.

Generally speaking, the breeding season is long for cottontails and varies depending on where they live. In temperate climate, breeding will begin in February and continue to September. Young, usually about seven of them, are born a month later, and like deer are called fawns.

Within two weeks the young begin foraging near the nest and will disperse after just another week. The mother will have been bred just hours after their birth, and the next litter is due very soon. The doe will have five litters before the breeding season is over. Young are sexually mature in a few months and can have young of their own before the summer is over; thus the term "breeding like rabbits."

Rabbit mortality is almost astronomical, and the high instance of breeding and producing fawns is essential to keep the species alive. Infant mortality is estimated to be as much as 75 percent, and experts believe most cottontails only live about 18 months. Most agree an adult rabbit rarely lives beyond three years.

In an unscientific study of my own, however, I believe there are instances where rabbits will easily live beyond the 18 months expected. During one winter in the early 1980s a couple friends asked me to remove some cottontails from their property. The property was inside city limits and the rabbits were barking trees and eating gardens in the spring. I provided the traps and both friends began bringing me rabbits.

I tagged each rabbit with homemade brass ear tags and turned them loose near my home. The rabbits' new home was several hundred acres of uninterrupted woods and brush, practically out my front door. Each rabbit caught was a full-grown adult at least eight months to a year old; some were obviously older.

Come hunting season of the same year, I hunted the area as I always do, but failed to kill any of the "tagged" bunnies, and thought maybe they had succumbed to bad weather or some predator. Then, during the next season, the tagged cottontails suddenly started showing up in front of my gun. These rabbits were still in the exact woods where I had released them. Most of these rabbits now had to be at least two years old, and some were surely three years and older. Although this was an unscientific study, it is obvious that cottontails can, and do, live beyond the 18-month norm.

The cottontail is a multifaceted creature. He is a survivor in every sense of the word. He has no defense against predators except to run, or sit motionless hoping he will not be spotted. As explained later in the chapter, "Why They Circle," his home turf will seldom be more than a few acres, and this he marks with secretions from scent glands under the chin. Rabbits rub these glands on rocks, saplings, fence posts, whatever is handy to mark their boundaries. (They also rub these on each other during mating.)

Did you ever have a cottontail run almost a perfect square pattern? This is the cottontail following the scent markers he has freshened many times before. When the dogs kick up and run one of these highly territorial bunnies, you can clearly see or hear them making almost perfect 90 degree turns. I've seen this many times, and the bunny is usually a pretty easy one to bag. Just follow the dogs down to one of the corners and take up a position there. If they keep up the pressure the bunny will soon be seen coming down his boundary line again.

The cottontail once lived in grasslands and open woods, but here in the eastern states he is more often found in cutovers and heavy thickets. He'll eat anything and can survive heavy snow and cold by barking saplings. Several rabbits can do heavy damage by chewing the bark all the way around valuable trees, effectively killing them. In tough times rabbits will eat earthworms, snails, and the bark of just about any tree or bush.

Raisers of domesticated rabbits know the rabbit voids two types of droppings, with one kind eaten again as a rabbit 'chewing his cud.' The second type of dropping is much darker and has had every bit of nutrient absorbed from it.

Most cottontail hunters know the rabbit carries many diseases. His entrails are a living host for many worms and parasites. Somehow he seems to live a healthy life despite these life-sapping organisms. Some cottontails, however, get so infested with tapeworms that they become noticeably smaller and weaker. Rabbits taken in open woods, high elevations, and throughout the cold winter months are more inclined to be free of most of these parasites. Proper cooking will kill all the germs in the cottontails' body, and hunters should not worry about the quality of the meat.

Veteran cottontail hunters will be familiar with one disease that is easily transmitted to man: Tularemia. Untreated, the flu-like disease can actually be fatal. Rabbits contract tularemia when bitten by deer flies. The tularemia bacterium is injected into the bloodstream by the fly and the cottontail then becomes a carrier. Hunters contract the disease when field-dressing infected rabbits, as the blood may enter through small cuts in the hands or under the fingernails.

Tularemia is not a pleasant affliction, and I can speak from experience, having had tularemia on at least two separate occasions. The good news is that it is treatable with antibiotics, and once stricken the hunter will rarely ever get it again. Unfortunately, it took two doses before I built up immunity to the tularemia virus.

Tularemia bacteria are likely to be killed in cooking, but rabbits known to have the disease should not be eaten. Affected rabbits will have very pronounced white spots on the liver, and the liver will look diseased and swollen. These will be much different from the small salt and pepper-like cysts associated with normal worm parasites. Hunters do not commonly find tularemia in rabbits because the bacterium quickly kills the infected bunny, but it does happen. Treat any suspicious rabbit with care and caution. Hunters would be wise to carry a pair of surgical gloves with them; however, I don't follow my own advice. But, I've already been infected.

As a carrier of all these parasites and diseases, and with hordes of predators stalking him, the lowly cottontail continues to thrive. His numbers are fewer than they once were, but huntable populations will be with us for many years to come. Call him Sylvilagus, swamper, rabbit, cane cutter, bunny, or little brown escape artist, but you've got to admire his adaptive personality. After hunting him for many years, and rousting him from a Ford Fairlane, I just call him, Mr. Cottontail!

Cottontail rabbits are more often found in cutovers and heavy thickets.

Aunt Mildred's is an unusual place to hunt bunnies, as you have to hunt around draglines, tri-axles, trailers, oil barrels, and an assortment of sediment ponds and other hazards.

2

HUNTING AT
AUNT MILDRED'S

The call was inevitable. It always came around the second week of November, and this year was no exception. "Hey Fish, how you doin'? Been doin' any huntin'?" Always the same questions . . . always the same answers. In fact, I could make a tape of the conversation, and we could each play it every November.

"Okay. Yeah. I've shot a few bunnies." Standard answer, but Joe knows I've been out every day and shot more than a few bunnies by now.

"Hey, why don't we go up to Aunt Mildred's Saturday?"

"Sounds good to me. About 8:30?"

Aunt Mildred's is a crazy place to hunt cottontails, and a special place for my buddy Joe and me. We get there only once or twice a year, but each visit is unique.

Joe's Aunt Mildred owns the farm. It's high in the mountains of Fayette County, Pennsylvania. It's not your average farm. Fact is, I'm not sure what they grow there; sometimes I think it's old machinery. They do have a few dairy cows, though, I do know that.

You see, Aunt Mildred's is a museum. Around the farm is a complete collection of rusting cars, trucks, relic farm machinery, hay wagons, tractors, bulldozers, junk, garbage, old furnaces, giant sawmill blades, boats, rolls of barbed wire, sheets of tin, collapsed buildings, old foundations, stacks of lumber, logs, and a variety of miscellaneous antiques. And that's not all. The farm is also in the process of being strip-mined, and the remainder of the standing timber is being cut for logs. It's an unusual place to hunt bunnies, as you have to hunt around draglines, tri-axles, trailers, oil barrels, giant machine parts, and an assortment of sediment ponds and other hazards.

Living in all of this stuff (mostly decades old and crumbling away) is an enormous supply of cottontails and their bigger cousins, mountain woods rabbits, which Joe and I affectionately call "great northerns." I'm not sure why this is so because Aunt Mildred's is actually south of us!

To give you an idea of what it's like to hunt in such a place, I'll try to describe an actual hunt there. Although it may be hard for you to believe, I swear on my Schrade Old Timer that it's all true.

First, it's a good idea to have a four-wheel-drive vehicle if you want to get around Aunt Mildred's. That's because tractors, milk trucks, tankers, and coal trucks do quite a job on the farm access roads. We also like to get far away from the hordes of dogs and cats that hang around the main house and barn.

Once out of the truck, our dogs waste no time sniffing out a rabbit. Joe, as usual, runs downhill to cut off the rabbit's normal escape route, and I head uphill for a cluster of holes under a small grove of cherry trees. The first rabbit is a smart one; he runs toward a small pond and through a flock of ducks where Joe cannot shoot. No matter; I kick up another just seconds later. It runs straight downhill, around some machinery, and jumps a small creek. Joe throws two and a quarter ounces of lead at him and calls the dogs. The bunny takes refuge under an unknown structure that surely stood upright at one time.

Joe's now screaming at the dogs, "Get him! Get him!" I break out a sandwich—this might take awhile.

Joe spends 20 minutes jumping up and down and tearing at the collapsed building. The dogs haven't been seen for 10 minutes. I decide to get ready. Yes, here he comes, up out of the basement with two dogs in hot pursuit. When he's clear of the dogs I let fly a load of 7 1/2s. The charge immediately clangs an old oil drum like a pair of cymbals. The rabbit sneaks out from under the drum and takes refuge in a huge barberry bush.

"He's in that bush, Joe. Get him!"

As Joe approaches, the rabbit rockets out of the bush and is followed by a swarm of hot lead. We finally take our first bunny.

We now work into a small apple grove complete with several vintage pickups and sedans, an assortment of abandoned farm machinery, and more unknowns. I check out several likely looking hiding places, look in the ends of a stack of pipes, and peer in the back seat of a few cars (cottontails like the soft seats).

I hear a dog yip a couple times, a shotgun blast, and look up just in time to see a great northern tumble out from under a hay wagon.

"Hey, good shot!" You can't give Joe too much praise or you'll never hear the end of it. Actually, it was a great shot.

As Joe's cleaning his northern, I watch the dogs squeeze under some long steel beams and the rusting hulk of a 60-foot mobile home frame.

"Uh, Joe, I see a bunny under there." Joe scoops up his gun (he hates to be left out of the action). It's too late as the swift bunny rockets out in a big hurry and rolls at the roaring sound of my 1100.

"Hey, good shot." Hey, good shot? Is that all? The guy never gives me any praise.

The next one's a classic. With the help of three sniffing noses, we trail another cottontail over 16 acres of old abandoned farm machinery and other scattered relics. The before-now-unseen bunny finally squirts out from some indefinable pile of steel and rust and quickly disappears under a nearby brushpile.

"Here! Here! Here he goes!"

The dogs go crazy, run around like idiots, and pay no attention to where I'm pointing. By the time they get their act together, Little Houdini has already slipped into the next pile, then into a third.

I'm screaming, "Here he goes! Here he goes!" But the dogs now look at me like I'm the idiot. No problem; I'll kick him out myself.

"Uh, Joe, he's in this pile right here. Cut off his escape uphill so he doesn't run that way."

He does anyway, right over Joe's feet and through more machines and equipment. Joe pulls down on the furry little beast.

"Uh, Joe, watch that coal truck! That's a good one." Joe lowers his Remington as the rabbit scampers under a Caterpillar (the metal kind) and over a discarded set of tracks (the metal kind).

It's hard enough to get the dogs on a fresh bunny track, but how do you get them to track over tracks? Now Joe's screaming, "Here he goes! Here he goes!" And hurts his foot kicking the tracks (the metal kind).

The dogs climb all over the dozer and miraculously pick up the tracks (the rabbit kind) and tear off toward another clump of brush piles. Joe scrambles after them. We have now pursued this rabbit for an hour and over and around 66 obstacles. I give up.

Joe's now patrolling around the stacks of brush, kicking the piles, and once again screaming, "Get him! Get him! Here he goes!" This is going to take awhile; time for another sandwich.

I'm just licking the mayonnaise from my fingers when the dogs start yapping with renewed fervor under one particular pile. Joe's been kicking and stomping on it like a maniac for 20 minutes. I get ready. Too late! Joe's 1100 barks and I see him scoop up the tenacious bunny. Good shot! But I don't dare tell him.

Joe steps back onto the rut of a road that splits the farm in two and takes the appropriate bows.

"Are you done fooling around? Can we get back to huntin'?" The guy's such a big ham!

We check out the edge of the strip mine and run a couple of rabbits around and under some fallen trees. We shoot a few shells but fail to claim any bunnies from the tangle. I'm quick to point out that the light's bad on this section of the farm, it's tough shooting through all these treetops, and that these particular rabbits are a new and speedier variety. Joe agrees with me for once and we drag the dogs out of the slashings. About three seconds later, we're both bogged down in ankle-deep ooze trying to cross the strips. The three dogs are snickering because they can gleefully walk over the slimy gray muck. After hunting with us, our dogs have learned to snicker a lot. Joe suggests we get out of the mud. I'll tell you, the guy's brilliant.

We stagger toward the truck, each of our legs encased in 20 pounds of clay. Just about the time we shake most of the mud loose, we step into piles of cow manure. The dogs start to snicker again. By the time we reach the other side of the pasture, where the truck is parked, each dog has had his turn rolling in the strained grass and corn. Joe says something about smelling something rotten. I told you, the guy's brilliant!

We drop off the rabbits at the truck, take a short rest stop (only for the dogs' benefit, of course), eat another sandwich, and descend on our last hunting spot.

This next section of the farm is unusual for Aunt Mildred's because it actually contains some real cottontail habitat, plus the normal discarded vehicles, machinery, and a huge garbage dump.

This time I take the easier downhill path. Joe leads the dogs into a small but dense thicket below a cornfield. The dogs are still behind Joe when his 1100 comes on in rapid fire. I notice weeds, small saplings, and leaves flying out in the thicket, but don't bother to swing up my scattergun. I mean Joe can't hit the Goodyear Blimp on a Sunday afternoon, but he rarely misses a bunny three times. I'm wrong, as usual, and a great northern leaps the tractor path right in front of me. I unsling the gun from my shoulder and throw a few ounces of lead at the fleeing target, but am distracted by Joe's screaming at the dogs.

"Get him! Get him! Here he goes! Here he goes!"

I figure this is going to take awhile and reach for a sandwich. A few pats around the old hunting coat and I discover a near emergency . . . I'm out of food! Now this is really serious!

Knowing Joe won't leave Aunt Mildred's without our limit of rabbits, I'm wondering if I'll have enough strength to make it back to the pickup, when the approaching dogs distract me. They're actually running the rabbit!

Joe and I look at each other and quickly spread out on the tractor path. We both know that if we don't take this rabbit, there will be no living with the dogs for the next two weeks.

Yeah, here he comes, afterburners blazing. Joe and I both open up on him about the same time, and the next thing I know Joe's yelling, "Hey, good shot!"

"Huh? . . . No . . . No, Joe. That's clearly yours, number four! Time to eat!"

"No way, that was really some fine shooting on your part."

Sure it was–I nervously pat my coat and vest again; not even an old, smashed candy bar.

"Okay, dogs, lets check out this powerline, dogs, good dogs!" Joe cheerfully calls out.

Nothing in my pants pockets.

We enter the powerline right-of-way and two rabbits go blasting out from a pile of brambles. Mine gets away cleanly, but I hear Joe's gun boom. Oh, boy, he's taken his fourth!

"Here dogs, here dogs. Here! Here! Here!"

The hounds short circle the rabbit in some kind of record time and it comes hopping right to me. I'm forced to shoot it.

While I'm cleaning the bunny, I notice the truck is just a speck on the horizon. I mention something to Joe about cooking one of the rabbits, and then come up with a good idea. Maybe he'll run out of shells!

"Hey, let's go check out the dump and those antique cars over there." This serves two purposes. First, it gets Joe turned around toward the truck, and second, we always do a lot of shooting in there. I hide the rest of my shells in my gamebag, then casually ask, "You think we have enough shells? I only have the three that are in my gun."

"Shoot! I always bring lots of shells when we come to Aunt Mildred's!" Swinging his coat open, Joe reveals a vest loaded with rows of shiny brass heads that looks like something Pancho Villa's men would wear. Yeah, great idea.

"I'm going to stay up here on the outside, you go ahead in there." Don't want to tell Joe I don't think I have enough strength to carry another rabbit.

Joe happily leads the dogs into the pile of trash and quickly opens up with the 1100. I'm not very optimistic. We've been in there before. The rabbits are a new species of "trash bunny" and offer only flashes and glimpses of themselves.

I find a nice stump to sit on and listen to the action. I start to hallucinate about T-bones and french fries. I even think I see the dogs chasing a Big Mac.

No, it's a rabbit! Before I can think, I pull up and shoot the Big Mac, I mean the rabbit. Oh, no, I've taken my fourth! Joe will never leave now!

Joe comes strolling over and gives me a dirty look. "Your fourth, huh? Boy, ran him around in there for awhile, never thought he'd leave the trash. Your fourth, huh?"

"Say, Joe, are we out of here, yet? We've taken seven bunnies. Here, take one of mine."

"Naaa, couldn't do that. Besides, we haven't even been in that group of Plymouth coupes over there yet."

By the time I clean my last rabbit and empty my gun, Joe has entered the next exhibit of "Old Autos Americana." I stagger over as Joe steps on a massive chrome bumper and walks nonchalantly across the top of a '44 Chevy (or maybe it was a '39 Caddy). The dogs have been squealing and yipping under the car for 10 minutes, while I recheck my hunting clothes for some unfound morsel. I figure this is going to take awhile, when a brown ball of fur, in an awful big hurry, exits a hole in the lid of the trunk.

What happened next appeared to be played out in slow motion. Joe, facing the hood, hasn't noticed the brown bullet scrambling across the trunk. He slowly pivots around at my yelling and screaming.

The gun slowly comes to his shoulder as the rabbit clears the bumper and hits the ground. BAMMM! A complete miss! The bunny, now in full stride, is on a dead run for the trash pile. BAMMM! The cottontail stumbles, definitely hit. I cheer, and he instantly regains his footing. Panic starts to set in. From my vantage point I can see that the rabbit will be out of range in just a few more strides. Visions of burgers and shakes are quickly being destroyed by each leap.

BAMMMM! The rabbit, hit in midair, tumbles and spins, suspended snail-like in an instant of time; then hits the ground like a rag doll.

Joe lifts his gun and hat to recognize the imaginary cheering crowds, slides down the side of the Chevy, then retrieves his trophy with a graceful bow. The guy's really a big ham.

"Speaking of food, do you think we can get out of here now? How about giving me a hand back to the truck. I've seemed to have sprained my ankle."

With the dogs tucked away in their cages, we collapse into the front seat. "Never drove my truck before huh, Joe? Good time for you to try her out!" (Don't want him to know I'm too weak to drive.)

"Boy, what a good day, don't forget to wave to Aunt Mildred on the way out. Ah, by the way Joe, how about stopping at the first McDonald's we come to."

3

BETTER FIELD CARE
MAKES BETTER EATING

My father wasn't much of a hunter. He had a full-time job, and was much interested in the sport. So, I began hunting with other boys in my neighborhood. Hunting in our area was, and still is for the most part, a time-honored tradition. Then, everyone hunted, or at least approved of it. Older hunters (in the 16- and 17-year-old range!) quickly took a couple of us greenhorns under their wing and got us on the right path. They showed us what to do, as they learned from still older hunters.

In the 1960s everyone was generally poor in our part of the country, and nothing was wasted. When we killed a rabbit, squirrel, or some other critter, every effort was made to get the thing into a pot. I strongly believe no piece of game should ever be wasted. If you or someone you know is not going to eat it, then don't shoot the animal. This pertains to doves, rabbits, frogs; there are no exceptions.

Today, hunting is still a rooted tradition here in my native Pennsylvania, but things are slowly changing. Negative attitudes about hunting are growing because of slobs who are called "hunters" just because they buy hunting licenses. Game is still plentiful, but much harder to pursue. Many landowners don't want hunters on their property any longer, and it gets tougher and tougher each season to find some out-of-the-way thicket where you can be left alone. Is it possible the hunter may someday be an endangered species? You bet it is, simply because private property hunting is slowly diminishing and game and hunting opportunities are slowly being pushed to smaller, public hunting areas.

What's all this have to do with learning how to clean a rabbit? It means there is no longer an endless supply of "older" hunters to hand down what they've learned over the years to fledglings who have yet to cast their first hound. New hunters often have to glean what they can from watching other hunters, trial and error, reading books, and viewing videotapes. So it is that we pass on a few tips about field dressing and cleaning rabbits.

I've learned to field dress all game almost immediately and keep it away from flies, dirt and, of course, any dogs we are hunting with. Flesh begins to deteriorate and bacteria starts to grow immediately after the rabbit is killed. Immediate field dressing ensures that few rabbits will ever be wasted. I've hunted with quite a few guys who didn't clean rabbits until the end of the day. Some rabbits were wrapped in plastic and shoved inside sweaty hunting coats for the rest of the day. In very cold weather I've seen bunnies freeze solid with the entrails still in them. Needless to say, I wouldn't eat any of the rabbits in either case.

Actual field dressing of a rabbit is an easy operation. I begin by plucking at the fur right at the apex of the breastbone until the skin begins to pull away. Continue pulling this strip of fur straight down the belly and all the way down between the hind legs and off at the tail. It's easy once you've done it a few times.

You now have a nice bare strip down the belly where you can see the entrails

through the thin inner skin. I hold the rabbit high up on his back and shake him slightly to keep all the entrails down in the lower belly. Using a small, very sharp knife (my favorite knife for this is a Schrade Old Timer normally called a "sharp finger"), pierce the skin at the breastbone, and using just the very tip of the knife slice the skin all the way down between the legs. Use just the very tip of the knife so as not to puncture the intestines. If the knife is razor sharp, as it should be, all you have to do is keep steady pressure back toward the opening and let the knife cut its own way. With a little practice you should be able to gut a rabbit in the dark and never cut the intestines. Don't get discouraged, however, as you'll make a mess out of one once in awhile, no matter how skilled you become.

Actual field dressing is easy and takes but a few minutes. Begin by peeling a strip of fur off the belly. A small, pointed, very sharp knife is a good choice. Split the bunny all the way through the chest and also split the pelvic bone.

14

Using just a couple of fingers, clean out the guts, carefully keeping the urine sack pinched close. The use of rubber gloves for cleaning out bunnies and any game is always a good idea, and if you would be comfortable using them, by all means do so. Powdered surgical gloves are available at most drug stores and are cheap to use; just don't leave used gloves lying around in the woods after you are finished. With some practice, you should be able to remove all the viscera with one hand while holding the bunny on his back with the other. Gutting the rabbit on the ground only gets dirt and debris all over it, and it pays to learn to do it in the air just by holding it.

Once the bulk of the guts are removed, split the chest up a little more (you'll learn to do all the cutting at one time after you get onto the procedure) and remove the heart, lungs, and windpipe. Next, while still holding the bunny on its back, split the pelvic bone with your knife. I've seen a lot of guys struggle with this and say, "I'll get that when I get home."

There are several reasons why I like to split the pelvic bone and clean everything out of the bunny right away. First, it saves me time and effort later when I get back to the house dead tired. It also gets rid of more waste and blood where bacteria can grow. Finally, it lets me leave the white jelly-like globules that are normally found at this end of the intestine buried in the woods, where my dogs are less likely to pick them up. The small, translucent globs that look like grains of rice encased in clear jelly are the larval stages of dog tapeworms. Don't let your dogs near them, or any part of the intestines.

The most effective way to keep the dogs away from the intestines is to kick a hole in soft ground and bury everything in there. Other times I may throw the entrails down old wells, in streams, or anywhere else the dogs can't get to them. I scold my dogs from day one not to eat rabbit guts, and they come to know that none of this is meant for them. My older dogs pay no attention to me while I'm cleaning a rabbit and usually go back to hunting in a few minutes. Aggressive pups on their first few hunts sometimes receive a sharp smack across the snout with the flat side of the hunting knife and are scolded severely.

Once the bunny is completely cleaned out, I may wash any blood off the fur with a dampened paper towel, then clean my hands with fresh water. This is one of the main reasons I carry a quart canteen of water while hunting.

Since bacteria flourish in a hot, sweaty, hunting coat, I prefer to hang cleaned bunnies from my belt where they can cool and dry. A long time ago, I used to slit the membrane between the large hind leg bone, the tibia, and the main leg tendon and slide them right on my belt with the body cavity out. This is still a good system. Another good way is to slit the same spot and attach a shower curtain hook through both legs and then attach it to your belt. Keep the open body cavity out away from you as you attach the hook and the same when you fasten it to your belt. This will keep almost all the blood away from you. Leather straps and bird hooks will also work, but the plain shower curtain method is hard to beat and was devised by me simply from trial and error.

Rabbits hung like this may bleed out the nose for a little while and may pick up a few leaves and weed seeds, but they are much better off than riding around in a plastic-lined hunting coat. "Hanging" them is also easier on your back and, as rigor mortis sets in and the bunnies stiffen stretched out, they are much easier to clean once you get them back home. Try it on a couple hunts and I'm pretty sure you won't go back to stuffing rabbits in your coat.

Keep rabbits as clean and cool as possible during the day. If the weather is warm, and especially if flies are still active, it's a good idea to plan on returning to the vehicle after a few hours and get any rabbits into a cooler or at least inside the car. Keep the car/truck parked in the shade and cover the harvest with a blanket or hunting coat. Advanced planning always helps. The "I'll worry about that once I get 'em," attitude doesn't lend itself to very good tasting rabbit or to the image of a conscientious hunter.

Rabbits hung out in the opening to dry will be easier to clean once back to civilization. I've never been fond of rabbits carried for hours inside a hot hunting coat. Some prior planning always helps. Remember we want to eat this thing!

Once home, try to clean the rabbits as soon as possible. I've fixed a place up in my garage with running water, a cutting table, and items needed to further take care of the bunny, and I use it for other game throughout the year.

One of the easiest tools I've found for taking off the feet and head is a large meat cleaver. Lay the feet on a flat piece of hardwood and in seconds the feet are gone. The head is also easily detached by a firm chop or by using the cleaver like a large knife. Cutting the head off after the fur is skinned down over it is another good idea, as it helps keep more hair off the meat.

Skinning is done in the air, again to keep as much hair as possible away from the meat. Hold the rabbit on his back and about midway down the belly begin working your fingers under the fur on both sides at the same time. Your fingers will soon meet each other; when this happens, grasp the skin tightly in both hands and pull hard in both directions at the same time. Ninety percent of the fur will come off with this one motion. Simply tear or pluck off the rest of the fur (usually some remains on the legs), cut off the head and tail, and wash the bunny off.

Next I'll wash or flip over the cutting board and lay the skinned bunny on top of it. If you want, you can use the cleaver to cut the bunny in two or into smaller pieces in seconds. Make one cut or chop directly in front of the hind legs, severing the hind legs. Flip this piece around and cut down the center of the tailbone, and you now have two separate hind legs. Go back to the main body, cut directly behind the last rib, and you now have four main pieces: the front shoulders, back, and two hind legs. I then slice the front legs off the chest cavity and discard it, as there isn't any meat there anyway. Wash the pieces thoroughly, then place them in a pot of warm salt water and let them soak overnight in the refrigerator. The next morning your rabbit is ready for cooking or the freezer.

There are, of course, many variations and many ways to clean a rabbit. The point of all this is to develop a routine and follow it. Field dress rabbits as soon as possible, then skin them and take care of them as soon as you return to camp or home.

I believe it is surely a sin to kill and waste rabbits, especially when they are excellent eating. When we shoot something, it ought not to be just for the sake of shooting it. If we are to be hunters and true sportsmen, we should surely set an example for those who are working hard to destroy hunting, and for the hunters that will come after us.

If you do not intend to eat it, or see that it gets to a person who will, don't shoot it. That goes for any game.

More recent dogs continue to carry on the tradition of great beagling. Pictured here is Run-em Over Tank with forty-four first place wins in several registries and several national titles.

4

THE ROOTS OF BEAGLING

No one knows exactly where beagling began. It is known that even in Egyptian times early craftsmen carved figures of hounds and hunts on pyramid walls. Drawings and carvings from the Roman Empire signify that this culture also enjoyed the sport of hound running. Then, however, it was a sport designed only for the rich, with large, blocky-headed hounds resembling large foxhounds.

Other early works from France and Germany depict hunters with hounds with all sorts of game: bears, foxes, small wolves (or perhaps coyotes), and smaller game such as hares. Somewhere around 56 B.C., Julius Caesar, in his quest to conquer the world for his beloved Rome, pushed his conquests into northern France and on into Britain. There is no doubt that with the Romans came many of their customs, including their recreational sports. Although it is generally known that there were already some good hunting dogs on the islands before the Romans, it is certain that they brought hounds with them for chasing game.

The Celts were another people who thrived during this time. Coming from central Europe, they settled the area of France (Gaul), pressed into northern Spain, and crossed to the British Isles probably in the 8th and 7th centuries B.C. They also sacked and burned Rome around 390 B.C. The modern populations of Ireland, Scotland, Wales, Cornwall, and much of Britain retain strong Celtic influences to this day.

By the time the Anglo-Saxons invaded The British Isles in the 5th and 6th centuries A.D., and drove the remaining Celts, and a lot of other people, from Britain, many of the dogs, and especially hunting dogs, were well established. Slowly, over the centuries, breeders began developing specific dogs for specific jobs. First, dogs were bred just for size. For instance: We need a dog to go down this hole and drag out game, so we will keep breeding these small dogs to these other feisty, small dogs until we get what we want.

Foxes were plentiful in Britain, so most of the larger, faster hounds were bred for fox hunting. Still, such hunts required horses, and for centuries only the affluent were able to participate in such sport. Slowly, however, the sport began to trickle down to those less fortunate in life. Again, it is not exactly known how this evolved, but it probably began when some "bad" foxhounds began to run off game (most notably, hares). Also, it is reasonable to assume that many smaller dogs discarded from fox hunting were used to start a new breed: The Beagle. It is believed that "beagle" came from a French word 'begle' for a type of hound that was used to hunt hares.

The actual beagle as we know it developed slowly because fox hunting retained such prominence among the upper class in England. It was more exciting to run a fox with all the pomp and circumstance of Master of Hounds, horses, and an occasional King or Baron thrown in for good measure. It was beneath them to run a lowly hare or rabbit. Eventually, however, the sport of chasing rabbits with hounds caught on with enough people so that a core of breeding stock was established.

It is generally agreed that almost every beagle in America was developed in England and later brought to the new country. In the English book, *Beagling*, by J. C. Jeremy Hobson (1987), the author writes, "The Royal Rock Beagles, whose country lies south-west of the River Mersey, were founded in 1845 and have the distinction of being the oldest pack of beagles still in existence anywhere in the world."[1] Hobson goes on to say that one of the first field trails there was held in 1891, and a few years later an organization called The Association of Masters of Harriers and Beagles was formed to keep track of stud books, and to run hound shows.

We have had to leave out many, many years of hound, and specifically beagle, development, but the beagle finally found its way to America. Again, because of poor or absent record keeping, these early beagles were assimilated into our society with little fanfare. Since the northern East Coast was settled first, it is logical to assume that the early dogs brought over from England were perfectly suited to running hares in Maine and other states. Early records indicate that these dogs were extremely well built, heavy boned, square-headed, and resembled foxhounds of the day.

It was somewhere during this time frame that the specific group of dogs called harriers sprang up. Harriers were well known in England even before fox hunting gained such widespread popularity. The name harrier is thought to come from the word "hare," for which the hound was used. Their description in many books, as miniature foxhounds, suggests strongly that the species (or correctly type), was downbred from the larger group.

Since I have mentioned harriers, I think it fitting that I should also mention bassets, the other dog always associated with running rabbits. Basset comes from another French word. "The basset hound is a long-bodied, heavy-boned breed of hound that stands roughly 11-14 inches at the shoulder and weighs between 40-60 pounds. Its long, soft, drooping ears, wrinkled brow, and short legs give it a distinctively wistful appearance. The breed is an old one and has been known for centuries in continental Europe, particularly in France and the Low Countries. Having better scenting ability than any breed except the bloodhound, it was used by royalty as a slow-working, steady trailer of game. Because it is low-slung, the basset hound is particularly good in rough, dense terrain. The breed has been known throughout the United States since the late 19th century"[2] . . . least you think the basset was bred 'down' from the beagle . . . it wasn't.

Let's assume now that all three breeds—basset, beagle, and harrier—are on the American shores. What happened next? Well, each breed is lost to obscurity in America for perhaps the next 100 years or so. Early reports describe the beagle to be "short-eared with snippy muzzles and crooked legs," not quite what we think of when we view our dogs of today. In the early colonial days, the sheer lack of numbers of dogs, and good breeding stock, possibly necessitated the breeding to other hounds especially the basset. Since the early hounds, or beagles in this case, had short ears and muzzles, these modified traits had to come from somewhere; the basset was the most logical choice. This is very obvious in the long ears, and short, stocky builds of many of our present-day beagles. In fact, this practice of cross-breeding beagles to bassets is still going on today.

As our country grew, and the settlers moved south and west into Virginia, Ohio, and beyond, the early colonists found cottontail rabbits in abundance. Now for practical reasons they no longer needed the bigger harrier, and foxhounds, that needed more space and more food. What they really wanted was the smaller beagle that was scattered here and there and gaining increasing prominence back in Britain. With new importations of "blue bloods" and hundreds of "grade dogs" being carried to all parts of The New World, the beagle was well on its way to finding favor in America.

In at least two books I have read, General Richard Rowett of Carlinville, Ohio is credited with bringing over the first "blue-blooded" beagles somewhere around 1870, although, as I have said before, many other harriers and beagles were here long before that. Rowett and his friends were interested in keeping to strict breed standards, and were interested in forming competitions for their dogs. His actions led to the forming of the American-English Beagle club a few years later. In November of 1890 in Hyannis, Massachusetts, the first American field trial was held. A few days later another trial was held in Salem, New Hampshire. [This and more can be found in *Hunting Hounds*, by David Duffey, ©1972.]

At about the same time Rowett brought to America his dog "Dolly", Mr. Charles Turner imported dogs by the name of, "Warrior" and "Sam," and Mr. Norman Elmore brought in a dog named, "Ringwood."[3] Almost every pure-bred beagle in America carries some blood from this early group, and they were the foundation for some early, famous strains. It is interesting to note that although beagles had been established in England for many years before they were in America competition, field trials in both countries began at practically the same time.

In some of these old books are old pictures and drawings depicting these early beagles with features of much bigger hounds. Most were heavy-chested, had large round bodies, and big, thick tails. Some appeared to have hair longer than that which we usually associate with our present-day beagles. In a very old photo that appeared in *The Beagle in America and England*, by H. W. Prentice (1920); page, 5, there is a picture of the very first field trial in Hyannis, Massachusetts. The picture shows about 13 hounds, many heavy chested, as I have described. Almost all are white with almost solid white bodies, with back spots placed on top of this white field. At least one, perhaps two, appear to be lemon/white or red/white. Even in these early American hounds, you can clear-ly see the characteristics of many of our hounds' ancestors.

Shortly after the Rowett beagles were imported, Capt. William Aston of Virginia brought over Imperial "Blue Cap" and Imperial "Blue Bell," which were actually the sire and dam of the Rowett beagles. Eventually, Mr. Hiram Card of Elora, Canada, secured these dogs from the Virginia kennel and, with other dogs he had either bought in The States or imported from England, he began the famous "Blue Cap" line. He insisted on his dogs carrying on the blue ticking and mottled markings of the parents. Even so, it is easy to see how these dogs were clearly related to the Rowett dogs being bred in Ohio.

In his book, *Wilderness Patchwork* (Second edition 1993), Willet Randall says he bought his first batch of beagles in 1896. I think it is safe to assume that these dogs were descendants from the first ones brought to America. We do know that from his first group of beagles, Randall had one dog, "Forest Patch," that was outstanding. Anyone who has had anything to do with beagling for any amount of time knows or has heard about Forest Patch. It is known that Randall bred to this dog many times, and it was the foundation for the "Patch" hounds still around today. Willet Randall apparently only had the dog for a few years, but the dog was already gaining immortality status, and Randall soon received many offers from people wanting to buy him. Randall refused all offers, but could not

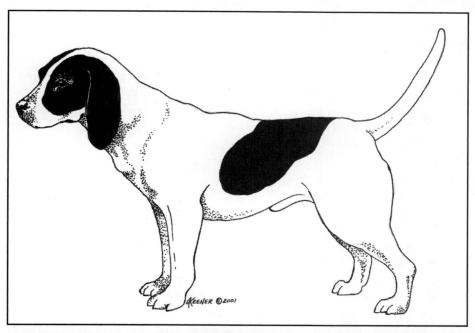

In 1896 Willet Randall began running and breeding beagles. Just a short time later one of the early litters produced a hound that stood out above all the rest – Forest Patch. After seeing him run for 19 solid hours Mr. E. C. Hare wrote about him, "I never hope to see his superior as a white hare hound . . . " Many hounds of today still carry on the "Patch" bloodline.

turn down his good friend, Ralph Butts, and reluctantly sold Forest Patch to him for $600 . . . a sensational price in 1900. Randall did reserve the right to exclusively breed to him.

In *The Beagle in America and England*, E. C. Hare of Holidaysburg, Pennsylvania, a famous beagler and judge of his day, wrote a chapter dealing with hare hounds and judging trails. Mr. Hare (I find the name very appropriate!) lists only three dogs that he felt were the best he had ever seen or owned, and one was Forest Patch. Although he does not mention Willet Randall, this was the same dog. The markings are identical, and Willet Randall mentions Mr. Hare's write-up in his own book.

According to Hare:

"I never hope to see his superior as a white hare hound . . . I have followed him for 19 full hours of continuous driving of the white hare in the Adirondacks of northern New York State. His shortest race was three hours and his longest race five hours . . . No man ever saw the day he couldn't put up a hare race . . . During those 19 hours of continuous driving he presented his hare to my view 100 different times . . . I have seen the hare 'wheel' him, 'angle' him, back-track, squat, hounds cut in ahead of him, overshoot the end of the drive by many yards while giving tongue in a feverish attempt to lead him—no matter, he has always been consistent in his work and clothed in a garb of hare sense, determination, courage, endurance, speed and ability to accomplish, he has stamped upon me his superiority as a hare hound over and above all that have been put down before me. Such a record could not fail to arouse in any sportsman the admiration for this splendid hound."

This is quite a testimony and it is obvious that Mr. E. C. Hare had much respect for the great Forest Patch. I often wonder what it would be like to have the privilege to see such a dog run, or gun over him, or to be part of a hunt that lasted 19 solid hours.

Those were much simpler times, and we owe a lot to those men who took part in the formation of our early beagles' roots. These guys were more concerned about improving the beagle breed, breeding outstanding individuals together to keep certain traits alive. Their culling of dogs was painfully harsh, but it only served to toughen the breed. If it were only so today.

In *The Beagle in America and England*, there is mention of a Mr. Doub, who must have been very prominent in the early beagle beginnings. It is reported that he never charged a stud fee, nor ever took any money for a dog. That's quite an accomplishment, one that is, sadly, unheard of today.

Finally, I must say that all this is just a tiny fraction of the information associated with our early beagle roots. A lot of information, and records of the early, good, or great dogs was never written down. It is clear to me that past hunters, breeders, and field trialers, besides loving their hounds, had one thing in mind: to improve the breed, be it harrier, beagle, or basset.

Although I am not an avid beagle trialer, it has been impossible not to hear about great dogs such Forest Patch, Luci Van Little Man, Glenn's Gay Demon, Fast Delivery Little Harvey, Flat Creek Joshua, and now Run-Em Over Tank, just to name a few. Tank is the first dog to ever hold the title of Champion in all three beagle registries: American Kennel Club, American Rabbit Hound Association, and United Kennel Club. His record, too extensive to fully list here, includes two ARHA National Championships, winner of two SPO, AKC Trial of Champions, two first place wins at The Northeast Federation in 1996 and 1999, plus state championships in Kentucky, Pennsylvania, and New Jersey. In total, as of this writing, he has 44 first place wins at ARHA, UKC, and AKC trials, unprecedented in the annals of trial history. Tank has also been selected as Purina's "Chosen of Champions," and has graced the covers of the national beagle publications six times.

Besides Forest Patch, I have owned progeny from all these great dogs. All of these dogs mentioned here are, and have been, great or exceptional dogs in their own right. We beagle owners and hunters are continually searching, breeding, and striving to find that one perfect rabbit machine.

Forest Patch arrived on the scene more than 100 years ago, and much effort has been expended to improve the breed ever since. But, I keep thinking back. Is there any dog alive today that someone could write: "No man ever saw the day he couldn't put up a hare race . . . During those 19 hours of continuous driving he presented his hare to my view 100 different times . . . he has always been consistent in his work and clothed in a garb of hare sense, determination, courage, endurance, speed and ability to

Mr. Dan Brinsky of Custer City, Pennsylvania, and the great Run-Em-Over Tank.

accomplish, he has stamped upon me his superiority as a hare hound over and above all that have been put down before me . . ."[4]

If there is, I have not heard about him . . . and he certainly doesn't reside in my kennel.

Notes:
1. J. C. Jeremy Hobson, *Beagling*, Page 67, (1987)
2. *Grolier Multimedia Encyclopedia*, 6th edition, S.V. "bassets."
3. *The Beagle in America and England*, (H. W. Prentice, 1920).
4. Ibid., 59.

It is the great runs with plenty of sweet beagle music and the special times that keep us tramping in brush year after year.

5

MEMORIES OF
OUR GREATEST CHASES

For the 30 years or so that I have been chasing cottontails, I've owned and hunted behind innumerable dogs. During this time I've killed more than 1,000 cottontails. Some were killed and added to the gamebag without much thought or fanfare. Some, on the other hand, were so elusive and gave the dogs such spectacular chases that we still tell the stories about them to this day. I suppose it is these great runs with plenty of sweet beagle music and the special times that keep us tramping the brush year after year. Following are seven unforgettable runs I had the privilege of being a part of. In searching more than 32 years of archives of my daily hunting journals, it is hard to pick out just a few stories, as so many are special. In some cases, I neglected to write down the names of the dogs I had with me at the time, and time has erased them from my memory. Some of the chases are so memorable I need no notes to recount them. I hope I can relate the stories in such a way that you, too. will feel part of the chase and part of the action.

Pine Thicket Run

It was late February 1984. It was cold and several inches of snow lay on the ground. Rabbit season in Pennsylvania had been over for several weeks, but occasionally I would slip over into nearby West Virginia and get in a few hours of hunting. As I climbed the mountain and pulled the truck into the pine thicket, I wondered what in the world I was doing here. The snow was ankle deep and the chance of getting any cottontails was remote.

The pine thicket was roughly 85 acres of Christmas trees in various stages of development. Most had been left unattended and were now large mature trees. Under these lived a few big woods cottontails that gave the dogs some nice long runs. Today would be one I would never forget.

The dogs, having been penned up for the last couple weeks, jumped from the truck gleefully, and didn't seem to mind the cold, six inches of white powder. We hunted the thicket for an hour or so when Sue-Sue, one of the best jump dogs I've ever owned, finally got up a rabbit. It was barely 1:00 P.M.

The pack went streaking away under the pines, but I knew they were in for a tough time. The pine tree thicket was broken into several blocks with access roads running around each block. It was on one of the roads that the cottontail was usually killed, as the dogs would eventually push him out from under the pines.

I took up a position at a four-way intersection of the roads, then decided to go along with the dogs and help them at the checks. I knew that once the cottontail jumped an access road, they were going to have a hard time in the deep snow.

The chase was going much better than I had hoped, and we were now halfway through the 85 acres and still going strong. It was 2:00 P.M. It was easy to help the dogs when they had problems and the bunny hit deep snow. This rabbit's large tracks and sweeping strides told me he was a tough old guy.

Around 2:30 P.M., the dogs, still in steady pursuit, had finally reached the far end of the thicket. I figured the rabbit wouldn't go any farther. As predicted, the hounds began a slow turn and came my way. I stayed out in front of them hoping for a shot, but the cottontail always jumped the blocks out of sight. For the next hour, the sounds of the chase slowly pressed me back to the main intersection of the grassy access roads, now covered with snow. I was just 50 yards from the truck.

At 3:30 P.M., I took up a position smack in the middle of the main intersection. I could now shoot in four directions. The chase had slowed considerably and I had my doubts if I would even see the quarry we had pursued all afternoon and over the entire 85 acres of snow-covered pines. But suddenly, there he was! In barely two strides the cottontail leaped the road I was watching and quickly disappeared into the next block of pines. No way could I even get the gun on him! At this instant I was sure he was gone for good. I stood there downhearted, and watched the dogs file across the tram, still trailing but exhausted. I thought about calling them off, but instead backed off the intersection and took up a stand watching the last remaining two roads on this end of the thicket. The rabbit must have also been tiring, and the dogs had considerably closed the distance between them.

Suddenly Mr. Cottontail dove out of the pines and ran into the wide intersection I had just left. The 1100 came to my shoulder and the blast seemed to shatter the ballet I had watched and heard all afternoon. The cottontail crashed headlong into the base of a snow-blasted pine. It was now 3:45 P.M. Fog and darkness would soon encircle the mountain and wipe away all trace of the play I had been privileged to appear in.

My dog Berries was 11 years old when she made this spectacular run, and this was her greatest season ever. The extraordinary cottontail was a huge mountain woods rabbit, and the 56th rabbit I had taken that season. He resides in my living room in full mount, a tribute to him and the dogs–Berries, Buster, and Sue-Sue–that brought him down.

The author with Omega (the last puppy in the litter!). All the greatest runs of memory always included great dogs like Meg.

The Stone Wall Chase

Joe Mikluscak and I had only hunted his aunt Mildred's farm a couple of times, but we had discovered many cottontails there. The place was laced with holes and a million other places for the bunnies to hide, and unless the kill happened quickly, the rabbit usually went to ground. Not so with one particular woods rabbit.

Joe and I were working through a particularly heavy thicket when the dogs suddenly cut loose. In those days Joe's male dog, Scrappy, and my female, Berries, were young and tough, but not noted for their trailing ability.

The bunny headed straight downhill and swung right. Since I was closer to the nearest tractor path, I ran for it. I got there just in time to see the big cottontail leap the road and enter a small hollow clogged with fallen treetops. The residents of the farm had cut a lot of firewood in there and the place was littered with logs, brush, and treetops.

Berries and Scrappy were in rare form this day, and Joe and I watched from the rim of the valley as the dogs climbed up and over every obstacle, neither letting the other give up on the scent. Berries and Scrappy liked each other and seemed to really enjoy hunting together. They finally pushed the cottontail out of the rough hollow and up along an ancient stone wall that formed the northeast property line of the old farm.

We caught up with the dogs about the time they were climbing a shallow place in the wall. The bunny had apparently gone over the wall and now only open woods and a large dish-shaped valley lay in front of him. Berries and

Scrappy continued the pursuit up the far side of the wall; Berries' fast chop–chop and Scrappy's low bawl told us the rabbit was not far in front of them. Then it happened.

Tired of being chased, the bunny made a sharp right and lit out for the valley beyond. Scrappy and Berries barely even slowed at the check and went streaking off into the timber. Joe and I were already nervous the dogs had left the property, but there was little we could do. This was Berries' and Scrappy's show and they would play it to the end.

We sat down on the wall, and talked about hunting and how well the dogs had trailed the rabbit. But by now we were both concerned. They had been gone for nearly an hour and out of hearing range for 45 minutes. We decided we would not wait much longer before searching for them. Just then we heard their faints cries somewhere in the valley. By all indications they still seemed to be trailing and perhaps heading our way.

"You don't think they're still on that same rabbit, do you Fish?" Joe asked.

"Sounds like it! Let's spread out along the wall. They're coming this way. At least we won't have to go look for them!"

Joe and I took up positions along the wall and the dogs kept coming. They were now bearing straight for us, but were a long way out. Suddenly I saw him coming. He was eating up yards with every stride and had pulled a good 150 yards ahead of the hounds. The timber was really open here, however, and even his great speed could not save him. Bammmm! The Winchester mildly rocked my shoulder and the big cottontail cartwheeled, his forward momentum sending him crashing into the wall.

Joe and I were elated and stood there admiring the rabbit. Neither of us could believe the chase, and did not move the cottontail until the dogs showed up to claim their prize. We stayed there a long time just praising the dogs and going over the great chase. It was one of the finest runs either of us had ever witnessed.

Scrappy and Berries proved to be a great team. In years to come they would have many chases together. Both dogs are gone now, but neither is forgotten; nor is the stone wall chase that happened on that chilly November afternoon in 1976.

Back Bone Mountain Hare

If you play golf, you certainly fantasize about being in a big tournament and making great shots like Tiger Woods or winning a huge check on Sunday afternoon. If you're a cottontail hunter, you fantasize about running snowshoe hares or giant swampers with your own pack of dogs.

About 100 miles from my home in West Virginia is a large section of the

Allegheny National Forest, and a place called Back Bone Mountain. There are hares on the Back Bone, and my cousin Bud and I made a couple trips there only to be buried under several feet of snow each time. We weren't hare hunters then and we had a hard time dealing with these big running rabbits and all the snow they thrive in. One fall, we decided to go immediately after the season opened in the first week of November to try to avoid the extreme snow conditions. We left for Back Bone Mountain on the morning of November 11, 1983.

We arrived in the area late on Friday afternoon, found a place to spend the night, then headed for the mountain. Our plan was to check out the mountain today, then hunt all day on Saturday.

At 3:00 P.M. we let the dogs down into six inches of fresh powder. We weren't too concerned about hunting, but wanted the dogs to have a chance to get out of their cages and take care of business. Just for the sake of it, we loaded the guns and followed them up the hollow.

The entire mountain was choked with laurel and huge rhododendron bushes. The rhododendron was so thick that it was not unusual to find yourself walking up and on the stems and branches. The stuff made the mountain a veritable jungle. Bud and I moseyed along behind the dogs, picking our way through the tangles, when the little rascals suddenly struck track. Neither of us had ever seen a snowshoe hare before, let alone a track, but from the large depressions in the snow we could only assume the dogs were running a hare.

Bud and I spread out about 60 yards apart and took positions in any decent opening that we could find. Sixty yards in this jungle may as well been two miles, but somehow I could see the tip of Bud's orange hat above the foliage on my extreme right. I was lucky enough to find a few table-sized rocks from which I could see a few small holes in the otherwise uninterrupted hedge of rhododendron.

I didn't know it then, but as hares go, this one wasn't a spectacular runner, and it's a good thing, as my hounds had never run a hare before. I was excited nonetheless to finally know my dogs were running a snowshoe, and we listened intently as the music echoed around the mountain and nearly disappeared.

I was nervous to hear my dogs so far off and in such rugged, unfamiliar terrain. But in a little while, I could tell clearly they had turned and were coming back our way. Better than that, the chase was coming straight for us. The dogs kept driving and soon they were nearly on top of Bud. It was then that I realized the hare had already gotten by him. Bud yelled something, but not wanting to give away my position to the big bunny, I didn't answer.

The dogs had gotten by us now, and were heading back down the hollow toward the truck. I spun around on the rock, and quickly the dogs made the turn near the road, and were coming back our way once more. Without any warning, I saw the brownish hare coming, slipping through each hole in the cover as if on skis. I swung on the next open spot and fired as he slid through it. He went down instantly.

A shrieking, Indian war hoop came next, as I knew I had finally taken my first snowshoe hare. Bud came crashing over.

"I know, he's a light beige color! I saw him slip by, but couldn't get a shot at him!"

Yes, the hare hadn't changed color totally, but was white on his rump, up the legs and around the ears, but he was a beautiful trophy to me.

We hunted the entire next day, but failed to kill any more hares. My dog, Berries, lived the entire 13 years of her life with me. She was one of the best hunting dogs I've ever owned. It was my desire to see her run a snowshoe at least once in her life, and this is what kept me returning to Back Bone Mountain. When the opportunity presented itself, she didn't let me down. It was my first snowshoe hare, but there would be many others in years to come. For Berries it would be the only one of her life, as just a year later she would be gone.

In any other case, this run would have been nothing unusual, but for Berries and me it was a special afternoon, and one of the greatest runs of both of our lives.

Two Rabbit Run

During the filming of my video, *Cottontail Rabbit Hunting*, we did an awful lot of cottontail hunting. And during the filming and hunting, we also had a couple spectacular and truly memorable chases, the kind that keeps all of us die-hard bunny hunters coming back for more. Some of these great runs were captured on video, although many times things just didn't work out and the real action escaped the camera lens. This is a run that didn't make it onto the video, but was a remarkable chase nevertheless.

Late in January 1988, a friend of my camera operator wanted to go hunting and perhaps shoot a few rabbits on videotape. Sean Sharp had lost an eye in a hunting accident about ten years earlier and really wasn't much of a rabbit hunter, but he took directions well and wanted to do everything he could to make the video successful. So we set out in search of cottontails on a blustery day in the middle of winter. In early afternoon, Sean jumped a big woods cottontail and held off shooting because we wanted to try to capture the run-back on film. He yelled for the camera—and, of course, the dogs.

In the wet, dripping snow the dogs found the trail easily, and tore off through the open woods. Knowing the area well, I felt this was going to be a quick and easy kill. I was wrong.

The hounds took the bunny up a brushy strip of saplings alongside the main woods, and finally into the open timber. Rabbits here usually went out this flat and turned around at the top of a steep hill. This time the bunny, sensing the pressure behind him, decided to drop over the hill and enter a large weed field in the valley beyond. From our vantage point we could hear the beagle music as the bunny looped the field a couple of times and suddenly started back up the hill.

The cottontail, now back in open woods, was destined to be immortalized on videotape when he suddenly made a sharp left and entered the brushy strip he had used to exit the area. In just a few seconds it was clear he was using the exact path he had taken the dogs out before. This is when the real excitement –keeping track of the rabbit's path by the dogs incessant barking–is generated for the houndsman.

The stage was now ruined for capturing the bunny on film, because he had veered away from the camera, and his fate for living a long life was improving with every second. Then he suddenly appeared. I threw up the gun and promptly blasted holes in the thick cover, with snow and leaves flying everywhere. But something was wrong; the bunny seemed to be in several places at one time, and I was having trouble keeping track of him. My third and last shell from the 1100 ripped into the snow as well. The rabbit was gone, but at least the dogs were coming!

We watched the dogs go by, still in good hot pursuit, then they swung back into the open woods. The entire pack suddenly slammed on the brakes–the bunny was there, stone dead.

Later that evening we studied the videotape, and discovered that somewhere, probably in the field, the dogs had picked up another rabbit and were pushing two ahead of them. I was actually shooting at two different rabbits and had miraculously hit one of them!

The chase was a great run and a special one for me, as it would be the last one filmed for the video after months of hunting. It would also be the last run for this great pack, the real stars of *Cottontail Rabbit Hunting*. Buster would soon be lost to old age and the ailments that accompany it. Sue-Sue and Howlley would eventually be sold.

Veteran beaglers and cottontail hunters will understand that good packs and good dogs never seem to be with us long enough, but in making *Cottontail Rabbit Hunting* and in great runs like this one, the dogs seemed flawless, like they would be together and with me forever. If it were only so . . .

Hard Top Bunny

In chasing cottontails for many years, it is hard to pick out certain runs or chases that stand out from all the rest. In most cases, the most memorable are ones where the dogs did a great job over tough terrain and the chase ended with a tumbled cottontail. Some are outstanding because of the time and distance involved or some unusual element that was thrown in. This next run had both and happened many years ago. Besides Berries, I can't remember what other dogs I had with me, but I remember they did an excellent job—almost too good.

I was hunting a swamp where I never killed many rabbits, but had some nice long runs. There was so much brush and cover in there that shots were tough to get, especially since most of the time I was hunting alone. This gave the rabbit only one hunter to avoid, and his chances of survival were pretty high. A normal chase in the swamp could last for hours and the dogs were constantly jumping and switching rabbits.

This day, however, would be a little different. The hounds locked onto a cottontail that made several passes around the swamp and then suddenly decided he'd had enough. With soldier-like precision, he jumped a small farm road and entered another brushy field, then ducked into a large standing cornfield. I was proud of the dogs' tenacity, but suddenly realized the chase was headed for a paved road a quarter mile away. No swamp bunny had ever run that far or crossed the road, and I was pretty sure this one would soon turn around. Wrong again.

Once inside the corn, the cottontail ran straight down one of the rows, taking the dogs with him. I was so far out of the picture by this time that it took me 20 minutes to catch up and break out of the corn. My heart sank when I heard the dogs several hundred yards across the hard top. By a stroke of luck none had been hit by a car trailing the bunny across the road.

The country road was not heavily traveled, but coal trucks and school buses occasionally passed by, and I strained to keep track of the dogs. I had few options. Should I pursue the pack and try to leash them? The brush was so thick in this uncharted field that pursuit was unlikely, and if I missed them and they suddenly turned back toward the road they'd have another risky crossing. I waited what seemed like hours, then the problem was suddenly resolved. The cottontail came streaking over the embankment and landed on the edge of the road, where it was met with a load of No. 7s. The rabbit fell right on the centerline! He wouldn't pull my dogs across the road again!

I quickly gathered up the bunny, stowed my gun in the weeds, and took up a position at the bottom of the embankment exactly where the bunny had come down. Arms and leashes were waiting for the trio of hounds as they tumbled down onto the edge of the road. A few cars whizzed by as I showed the beagles their prize. With the bunny down, they were content to follow me back to the swamp.

The author admires a nice cottontail taken after a particularly long and exciting chase. Sometimes it's not the size of the quarry, but the method and the circumstances needed to see the hunt to completion.

Lake Geneserath Hare

On my very first visit to Beaver Island, Michigan, I saw some of the best dog work and a few of the greatest runs any rabbit hunter could ever hope to enjoy. One was so special I still relate to it this very day. It was October 1993, I had already hunted two days, and my plane was leaving on Wednesday (two days hence). I was flying directly from the island to Traverse City, so Tuesday was my third and final day of hunting.

One aspect that makes this run so unusual for me was that I had none of my own dogs with me. Since I had flown in to meet a few guys, bringing dogs with me was not very realistic. I had only known Holly Wolfe for a few days and was unfamiliar with his Gay Demon bred hounds and how they ran. Holly had just gotten into beagling a few years earlier, and although he wanted the dogs for trialing, they were really unsuitable for the job. These guys were hunters! They could smoke a rabbit!

The morning went well, with us taking seven snowshoe hares. After a brief lunch at lakeside we strapped a couple beepers to the hounds and set them loose along the southwest side of Lake Geneserath. In no time the hounds picked up a hare track and streaked away to the south, all five dogs screaming at the tops of their lungs. They accelerated rapidly as they went around a big crook in the lake shore and almost out of hearing. It was an incredible chase covering hundreds of yards in mere minutes. Now the pack, in full cry, slowly began a big arc to the left and back toward us.

On the first pass, the hare circled our position but not close enough for any one to get a shot. Holly Wolfe was carrying a .410 pistol and had tried for two days to kill a hare with his new hangun. I just stood there in awe, listening to this spectacular hare chase. Each dog's voice blended into one musical hymn, with the beepers ringing above the chorus. It still gives me tingles just thinking about it.

To this day, I can still hear those hounds screaming and those beepers ringing a half a mile away! Even after hunting hares for the next eight autumns it is still one of the greatest runs I have ever seen while rabbit hunting.

The pack took off down the left side of the lake again, beepers and dog music marking every step of the way. For twenty minutes they went completely out of hearing range, then methodically marched back up the shore of the lake. The dogs were locked onto this rabbit and nothing would shake them. The hare got past Holly, then sprinted across the sandy opening I was watching, just out of shotgun range. It looped around Scott, one of the members of our hunting party, and he missed twice.

I tried to intercept the bunny on his return trip, but he got around me. At one point I could see him under the open pines, with the dogs in hot pursuit. For a short time they were even sight chasing him! He spun around the giant lake one last time in an absolute, desperate attempt to elude the dogs. Finally, completely exhausted, he hopped into full view of Holly's .410 Contender. Holly finally killed a hare with a pistol!

"That hare had had it," Holly said. "One more pass around that lake and they would have caught him!"

There was no doubt about it. If Holly had not ended the chase, the dogs would have run down the hare. This pack of Gay dogs was thrown together just a few weeks before the hunting trip, and neither Holly nor anyone else knew how they would perform. But the team acted as if it had been running together for years. I was so impressed that I spent a small fortune and bought two Gay dogs a few months later. To this day, I can still hear those hounds screaming and those beepers ringing half a mile away. Even after hunting hares for the next eight autumns, it is still one of the greatest runs I have ever seen while rabbit hunting.

The Crab Apple Flat Run

It's funny how some memorable runs, or chases, sort of just come about. Unexpectedly, nothing planned, they just happen. It's also a little disappointing when your dogs work and run like world class hounds and you're the only one there to see it.

I dropped the dogs, Ralphie, Lightning, Annie Oakley, and the new pup Sherri-Red, from the tailgate and started around the dirt piles bulldozed onto the end of the lot. A new house under construction stood to my right. The owner had been working on it for the past couple of seasons, and it was nearing completion. The house was still unoccupied, but I knew my hunting days in this great bunny thicket would someday come to an end. It was November 25, 1991.

We had been out of the truck for less than ten minutes when the dogs started a bunny at the base of one of the dirt mounds. I didn't see the bunny, as he must have lit out at the sound of our approach. No matter, Ralphie said it was a good, hot trail and the dogs soon disappeared into the thicket. I moved slowly forward, taking up a position just fifty yards off the nearly cleared lot. The rabbits here still acted as if no house was there, and I expected to see the bunny come back through the new lawn.

The dogs slowly locked onto the track and worked out to the right of the U-shaped thicket. The thicket was at one time nearly a square, but the new home and lot had cut about a two-acre hole into it, creating the upside-down U shape. The dogs now turned to the right and entered the thicket to the right of the house, an area I always called "the flat." The flat was a nice flat area about three acres in size that I had always envisioned as an excellent spot for a home, and a place where over the years I had killed many bunnies.

The beagles zigzagged through the flat and slowly turned my way. I saw the big woods bunny coming, gliding along the edge of the new yard.

"Darn, I'm out of range. And he's heading for the wood pile!" I said to myself. "That's it. This run's over."

I saw the cottontail disappear behind one of the woodpiles and was sure he had gone into it. The woodpiles were cut firewood left over from clearing the lot.

The dogs came out through the yard and I casually showed them where the bunny was hiding, figuring they'd go search out another when they saw the bunny had holed up. Instead, Ralphie let out a chopping bay and started straight up one of the rocky mounds. The other dogs joined in and the chase was on again.

Now the dogs were on the left side and bending slowly into the base of the U again. I knew the bunny would head for the flat again and decided to hold my ground by the woodpiles, figuring he would probably run the same pattern once more. He didn't, and I was kicking myself later for moving from my first stand.

Coming out of the crab apples and up the slight rise to the entrance of the flat, the dogs lost the trail. Five minutes went by, then ten.

"Come on girls," I thought. "Someone find that trail. You know where he's going!"

With that thought, Lightning let out a shrill, piercing bark, then another. The rest of the dogs chimed in and blasted into the flat.

Once a run heats up and gets good, I get really intent on killing the rabbit. When everything clicks and the dogs work hard, I believe they want you to get the bunny and are excited when they pull up to the kill site and you're holding a fresh cottontail. It keeps them excited and interested and they love the praise and petting they get after a nice run. I've heard the stories about never having to kill a rabbit in front of a dog for him to be a great hound. Maybe, but I've raised and trained a lot of gundogs, and they just seem to get better with the more rabbits you kill over them.

So I was intent on killing this bunny and was scanning the brush thoroughly when I saw him again. He wasn't edging the yard this time as before, but instead was slipping out of the flat and heading back down into the main crab apple thicket. He would pass by only a few feet from my original position.

"Man, I should have stayed put. How stupid. I'm never going to kill this bunny!" I thought to myself.

The dogs were having trouble with the line and lost the trail at least three more times in the next 45 minutes. Lightning got them back on once or twice and Ralphie found the trail at least one time. I wondered how long before they lost the trail for good or the bunny got tired and holed up somewhere. I'm not sure why they were having trouble sometimes and running so well most of the time.

The bunny had looped the thicket and was back in the flat. I had jockeyed around and was now standing midway between the woodpile and the main thicket. I had seen the cottontail at least three times, always out of gun range.

The chase traversed the whole flat for one last time and the bunny swung hard left. He was back in the main thicket now at the base of the inverted U. The dogs were way behind him, coming down the right leg out of the flat.

Now I saw him sneaking back up the left side toward the mound where he had been jumped. He was running the exact path he had taken earlier, only in the opposite direction!

When he got out of sight again, I half ran, half-tiptoed back to the woodpiles. And here he came, around the mound about eighty yards out. At about fifty yards, he slammed on the brakes, stood up, and looked my way. Thinking the rabbit had surely seen me, I threw the gun up and pulled the trigger. He flipped into the air several feet, then hit the ground in full stride, angling slightly left and somewhat closer. He was in good gun range now, and the 1100 hurled another casing into the air.

The rabbit leaped straight up again, turned and ran off into the heavy brush at the base of the mound. I ran around the woodpile and crashed in after him. I figured he would surely go to some type of hole or sanctuary, but there he was, lying just out of sight.

He was a big cottontail, a big woods bunny, one of the nicest I've ever taken from the thicket. The dogs took their time getting to me, and for several minutes I admired the beautiful rabbit. He was at least three years old, and I wondered how he had eluded me and my hounds the many times we had hunted through there. I also took a good look at the thicket, and the shadow of the house I was standing in. For twenty falls I had clawed my way into this thicket and knew every sapling, tree, and log, I was sure I knew the thicket better than any person on earth. How much longer would I be able to hunt or walk there?

I shook those unpleasant thoughts from my head, showed the bunny to the dogs, and praised them for their great work!

A few minutes later I hung the cottontail in a cherry tree to cool, and started toward the main thicket.

"Let's go dogs! Let's see if we can find another one-it's getting late."

There are so many others. Hare runs in New York with Zef Selca's Swiss hounds, chases over tough, thorny terrain in Greene County, Pennsylvania, and many others where the bunny was never killed. But the runs and chases that stand out always seem to be the ones that involved a particularly large and crafty woods bunny, be it hare or cottontail. I am surely naive in thinking this way, but it was as if his destiny was to encounter the dogs and me on his last day on earth. It's almost like he lived his entire life for that one special afternoon, just as if he were put there for me and the dogs and the brief time we all spent together. It is this feeling that makes me respect the little critter so much. And when I heft my next one and admire his sleek appearance, his finely textured fur, and his tenacity for life . . . may I never lose this feeling.

The runs and chases that standout always seem to be the ones that involved a particularly large and crafty woods bunny . . .

6

HARD TACK CANDY

H ubert was a farmer all his life. Things were simple back in the 1950s when he was growing up. You got up early, milked the cows, took care of what you had to do, then went to school. Later, when you got back, Dad would be in the barn with the cows, and he would give you the "look" when you got there, because he thought you fooled around somewhere for longer than you should.

Hubert Sr. never said too much; he was a quiet, unassuming guy. He didn't take any lip from anyone, and you better not give him any either. Yet, he always seemed to be there when someone was in trouble or a neighbor needed some hay brought in during an illness or something. He was a strict father, but fair. He must have been a youngster at some time, and he barely said anything when young Hubert ran the old "H" tractor through the north wall of the shed. Young Hue wanted to keep it quiet, but Dad was there just moments after it happened. He didn't say anything, just gave Hue the "look," but was secretly seen smiling as he pulled the boards away to free old Bess. It was though the same thing happened to him somewhere along the path of life.

Hue was now Boss of the farm. His dad puttered around the house, and took his usual place on the front porch to smoke his pipe and look over the work being done. From his perch, he could see almost everything across the valley. And once in a while Hue would see him scowling when he thought something ought to be done the way he used to do it. Hue was respectful, but things were different now. The farm, although the picture of prosperity, was in trouble. Prices for milk, eggs, beef, everything, had barely moved in ten years, while fuel, tractor parts, and the like had gone through the roof. More and more land had to be plowed, more cows had to be milked just to stay even. Hue had two hired hands now, but knew he could not keep them much longer. He was in debt up to his eyebrows; farming wasn't much fun anymore.

Hue had the hay wagon backed up to the barn with the huge dual-wheeled John Deere, and was methodically placing bales on the conveyer powered by old Bess. John, one of the hands, was somewhere inside the loft stacking. A newer pickup pulled silently up to the tractors. Ordinarily, Hue would barely have looked up, but it was Barry from down the road. Hue liked Barry. Barry would stop for no reason sometimes, throw a few bales, help milk or just sit on the porch and chat with old Hubert. Hue was not sure what Barry was all about. He was the new breed—worked in town, leased his land out to farmers still willing to till and cut. Hue knew he had a bunch of dogs. Heard them running sometimes in the lower fields. Barry was a little different from the others that worked in town; he didn't seem to want anything. Yeah, that was it. Barry didn't expect anything back for his generosity. Hue liked Barry.

Barry said, "Hi" cheerfully, muscled Hue out of the way, and began placing the bales on the belt. Hue was annoyed; "I'm quite capable of doing it," he thought to himself. So that Barry would stop doing his work, Hue cut the power on Bess and turned the key off on the Deere idling nearby. The silence was almost deafening.

"Hey, I'm glad you did that," Barry almost yelled. "I wanted to talk to you anyway. Remember I told you I had that litter of pups? Well, that guy at work wouldn't take that nice female I had been saving for him. Said his wife wouldn't let him keep no dogs. It's pretty bad when the Mrs. runs the show, huh?"

Hue nodded, but said nothing. He had no idea where Barry was going with this.

"Anyway, she's getting a little too old to sell for a pup. I thought I'd bring her over tomorrow and give her to you."

"You must be crazy," said Hue. "I ain't got time for no dogs over here! Man, I'm working 18 hours a day to keep John and Lou movin'. I ain't got time for no dogs. That worthless shepherd has been dead nearly two years. I don't want no more dogs!"

"Ehhh, you don't do nothing but work over here! I haven't seen you so much as crack a smile in a month. I'm bringin' her over tomorrow," Barry said, climbing back into the pickup.

"I don't want no dog. Don't bring her!" Hue waved his hand almost vulgarly at the truck as it pulled away.

Hue didn't think very much more about the episode. And Barry didn't show up the next day.

On a cool September morning a few days later Hue was on the way from the morning milking when Barry pulled in. The local milk hauling company had just told Hue they were going to have to raise the price two cents per gallon, and he was not in a very good mood at all.

Barry, his cheerful self, hopped out of the pickup. "Hey, how's it goin'? I was off today, thought I'd bring the pup over!"

"I told you I don't want no damn dog! Take it out of here!"

Barry acted as if Hue hadn't even spoken, just reached around his back and thrust the little black and tan pup into Hue's arms. Hue, angry, tried to say something, but Barry slammed the door. It was too late, Barry was already driving away.

Barry acted as if Hue hadn't even spoken, just reached around his back and thrust the little black and tan pup into Hue's arms. "Well, I got to get goin'. Let me know how she makes out?"

Hue, angry with Barry, tried to say something, but Barry slammed the door. He tried to open it, but the pup was already squirming in his arms and digging for something in his pocket. Hue, not without heart, grabbed at the pup, as it was about to tumble out of his arms.

"Hey!" he yelled at the truck, "You said this dog was too big to sell! She's no bigger than a corn nubbin!"

It was too late, Barry was gone and the pup was already aggravating Hue, still drilling for something in his pocket. Hue dug down into the material and came out with an old piece of matted hardtack candy. The pup took it excitedly and beat its tail against Hue's chest. "What am I gonna to do with you?" he said quietly to the little beagle. "I don't have time for you." The pup just rolled the candy from side to side, and continued to beat its tail. But slowly, as the little female squirmed and dug into Hue's chest, that little smirky smile cut across his mouth, like old Hubert when he saw Bess sticking out the wall of the shed. When Hue got to the porch he still had the pup tucked under his arm. Old Hubert didn't say a word, just smoked his pipe and watched as Hue laid the pup beside him. "Here, watch this thing. You're not doin' anythin' anyway!"

The screen door slammed behind Hue and the smirky family smile spread over the old man as the smoke spun around his head. The pup just kept licking and playing with the hard tack.

The next morning Hue noticed new feed pans on the porch. One had been licked clean and the other one was now filled with water. Hue looked at the shiny new pans with a puzzled look.

"Barry dropped them early this morning before ya was even out of bed," the old man spoke up from his chair. Hue thought that was a dig for sleeping in five minutes longer than usual; but was wondering more about where the dog was.

He didn't say anymore, just started for the barn to begin milking. John and Lou were already ushering the cows into the slots. As Hue reached the barn door he saw something small and brown following him. His smile widened as he saw it was the pup, and then shot a quick look at his dad to see if he had noticed. The old man puffed away and gave no hint that he saw anything.

The pup was a nuisance all day. It got under foot. It rolled in manure. It almost got trampled twice, and if it weren't for Hue's interference it wouldn't have made it through the morning. Later that evening, when the afternoon milking was done, Hue headed for the house. This time there was a little spring in his step. When he got to the porch, he saw that the feed pan had been filled again. He didn't say anything, but ate the big supper Margaret made for him and went to bed.

The next morning Hue stepped off the porch and looked around. The pup was not around but the food was gone again. Hue said a muffled 'good morning' to Dad and stepped off the porch. He took a few steps, looked around, and called softly, "Here, Candy!"

The pup didn't come, and Hue shot an embarrassed look at his father. "Here, Candy! Let's go milk!" he called louder. "Candy" came flying around the corner of the old farmhouse and ran between his legs. Hue didn't look back, but could hear choking and coughing from the porch.

From then on Hue and Candy were rarely apart. She rode on the hay wagon. She chased the chickens. And she became an expert at avoiding those nasty cow hooves. Hue began carrying hard tack in his pocket for her.

As fall faded into the gray skies of winter the young, bouncy puppy grew into a sleek, muscular, full-grown hound: beautiful black and tan with a tiny white tip on her long tail. Hue took her with him in late fall as he brought in the last cutting of hay. She would ride beside him on the seat he fashioned on the fender of the John Deere. It wouldn't be long before a cottontail would bounce out of the hay. Hue would stop the tractor and tenderly place the anxious beagle on the track. Off she would go in full bay into the next field or the woods beyond. Hue liked farming again.

Barry continued to stop in, but took little interest in the pup. He would remark about Candy's good looks or the fact that he heard her running a few times while Hue was cutting hay. He more enjoyed Hue's new attitude. Even though the farm was still in financial trouble, Hue took it in stride. He had to sell off a few acres to more city folk, and he knew that the farm would someday be consumed by the urban sprawl creeping in from all directions.

One evening, almost two years from the day Barry drove in with Candy, as Barry was running his dogs in the local swamp, he suddenly heard a new voice in the pack. He recognized it as Candy and a few minutes later Hue walked around the corner of the trail.

"Hi Hue!" Barry said happily. "I didn't know you came in here."

"Oh, I don't usually. I heard your dogs running clear from the porch. Candy about broke my arm until I got the tractor and rode down to the west corner. She made a beeline for those dogs when she heard them."

The men watched the dogs for the next two hours. They came across the trail many times, Candy tucked tight in with the rest of the pack. Barry made comments about this dog and that one . . . and how Candy picked up that last check. Hue didn't have any idea what he was talking about, but he loved to hear the pack running. Finally Barry spoke up.

"That's a fine dog, Hue. I'm going to a big trial on Friday. I know you never sent in Candy's papers, but I did. I have them at home. You're welcome to go along and bring Candy."

"Naaaaaaa, I've got cows to milk, you know that. I had to lay Lou off last week."

"Well, I understand. Would you mind if I take her then?"

If it had been anyone else in the world Hue would have said no immediately. Candy was his security blanket. Now that Dad was gone, Candy had even taken over his spot on the porch. Hue hesitated for a long moment.

"Yeah, sure, take her," he said in a low voice.

"Don't worry, Hue, she'll be fine. I'll bring her back bright and early Monday morning."

Hue moped around all weekend doing his chores on automatic. With Dad gone, Margaret would come out on the porch and take Candy's chair. "She'll be fine, Hue. You know Barry wouldn't let anything happen to her. She might even be having a good time running with all those dogs."

The weekend went extra slow, and Hue was up even earlier than usual on Monday. He was milling around looking out the drive before even going to the milk barn. Margaret peered out the window, smiling and watching Hue pace.

Finally Barry's shiny truck rounded the corner and pulled up near the front porch. As Barry opened the door, Candy jumped over his arm and onto the ground. Barry was not sure who was happier, Hue or Candy.

Barry didn't say much, just reached in the cab and brought out the biggest, shiniest trophy Hue had ever seen along with a fluffy blue ribbon. Barry laid the trophy gently in Hue's arms.

"Oh, by the way, there was a cash prize, too. It's a tidy sum," Barry said placing an envelope in Hue's side pocket.

Hue couldn't speak, but Barry could see the tears welling up in his eyes. Margaret began sniffling on the porch behind them.

Hue looked at Barry with deep appreciation, not for the trophy, but for bringing Candy into his life. He still couldn't speak, and Barry was already climbing back in the truck.

Hue turned to the house and the sleek brown dog followed as always. The cows could wait. Hue walked into the huge living room and carefully placed the trophy on the floor as he cleared the place of prominence in the middle of the mantle. He wiped the spot clean, and adjusted the trophy and ribbon until all were perfect. Then he reached in his pocket and gave Candy a piece of hard tack while he swept her into his arms. Candy licked his face as she rolled the hard tack back and forth in her mouth. Margaret watched from the kitchen doorway.

Finally Hue was able to speak. "Let's go milk, Candy!"

That was the only trial Candy ever attended, and Hue never asked Barry for any of the details. Barry only said, "She's a fine dog. I had several guys offer big money to buy her." Hue already knew that. Sell her? That would be like selling Old Bess . . . or his right arm.

As the winters unfolded, Hue took Candy hunting many times, collecting a few rabbits with Dad's old single barrel. Candy loved hunting, and while Hue was with her he forgot about the houses and stores creeping closer and closer to the farm. He had to sell a few more acres to keep the farm going. He knew that someday he would have to sell it all. But for now there was peace and the beautiful bawl of Candy coming up through the apple orchard.

The author's cousin George Dye with Buster, an exceptional male dog. The author prefers female beagles for all-round rabbit hunting.

7

SELECTING A BEAGLE
MALE OR FEMALE?

I f there is one question I've been asked over the years more than any other, I'd have to say it is: "Which makes the best hunting dog, the male or the female beagle?" In fact, the question has been asked so often that I felt it was important enough to include a segment about it in my video, *Cottontails & Hares*.

Well, for me there is a very simple answer. Here's what we said in the video and my opinion hasn't changed a bit.

"Without a doubt the females make the better rabbit dogs. Now before you start writing us a letter, we know there are plenty of exceptions and we've owned some great male beagles, but in general, and most of the time, the females will be the outstanding dogs. Females are much gentler to handle, are less likely to fight with other dogs . . . they usually listen better, and stick more to the business of hunting.

"Male dogs fool around a lot more, kill valuable hunting time by marking every tree and bush–and are always looking for–well, you know . . . girl dogs!!"

It's true. The outstanding dogs always seem to be the females. Oh, they are never given the credit, and this is mainly because they can't be put "up for stud," but when I'm on a serious rabbit hunt, sometimes many miles from home, I know "my girls" are going to come through for me and do the very best they can.

With a male, you never know. Is he going to spend the day smelling a female coming into heat? Or is he going to waste a lot of time peeing on every thing the other dogs touch? Is he going to fight with my new friend's male? You bet he is.

In all fairness, I must say I've owned a few good male beagles. Buster and his son, Ralphie, together gave me more than 15 years of service and loyalty. They were valuable hunting dogs, always leaders of the pack, listened to me extremely well, and I wanted them on every hunt. They were, however, exceptions in my book. It is also true that a good, aggressive male beagle will bring fire and leadership to an otherwise lackluster pack. Of course we need good male hounds, but in most cases the males simply do not perform up to the standards set by the girls.

I believe that the female beagle has a special attraction for her male hunter/owner. I'm not sure I can really explain this, but it is definitely there. There isn't anything bizarre implied here, but the attraction between males and females is one of the strongest in the universe. I'm positive she senses the fact that I'm male, and she's female. This male/female bond can become quite strong and the dog simply learns to do everything she can to please. In the hunting field this equates to hard work and extra effort. She wants to do her very best and loves the praise and attention she receives afterwards.

Females also seem to have more energy and will ignore some pretty serious injuries to keep hunting. They will "play hurt" much more so than a male dog will. I've owned, trained, and hunted a pile of dogs. Every one of them was different or special in some way. I wouldn't have given up Ralphie for any amount of money, but on his best day he couldn't outhunt Lightning or Annie Oakley.

Male dogs get all the glory, their pictures grace the covers and pages of every hound publication in existence, and yes, there have been some great ones. It is my opinion, however, that many of these males were pushed and pampered by an owner whose goal was to make a name for himself, and to eventually advertise the dog at stud, heralding all his past "accomplishments." Some of these males would have been almost worthless on a rabbit hunt, but that is another subject.

The male receives all this recognition and glory because it is believed his sperm carries the majority of the genes passed along to his offspring. Have a champion male, have a litter of champions. If it were only that easy! It's a fallacy. The dam has just as much influence on the traits passed along to the puppies as the sire does, and in some cases even more. This is not known until the pups are grown and evaluated. But, it sounds simple: "I've got this champion male, send me your female, I'll charge you a big stud fee, and you'll have a whole bunch of carbon copies." I said it sounds simple . . . it isn't.

Which is the better hound, the male or the female? If you're interested in stud fees, and the notoriety that a male beagle could possibility bring you, buy a male. I'm interested in rabbit hunting, and I'm putting my money on the girls!

8

BEAGLE TRAINING

Training a beagle to run rabbits is not that difficult providing the dog comes from unchallenged hunting stock. In my opinion, however, a beagle is more than just an instrument to run bunnies. If a dog is going to hunt with me, and possibly take up residence in my kennel for many years, that dog is going to have to know a few other things: come when called, hunt in the direction I want to go, ride and travel easily, obey a few simple commands, and generally behave himself. In addition, he/she must do his/her part in trailing rabbits.

The beagle is not one of the smartest breeds on earth. His single-mindedness toward running rabbits makes him a superb hunter, but this tunnel mentality makes it difficult for him to learn much else. Where a beagle is concerned, training can be summed up in one word: repetition. The trainer, in most cases the new dog owner, must practice each command and new experience over and over again until the dog accepts it as part of his natural behavior.

Actually, I've never considered myself as an honest-to-goodness dog trainer. In my own humble way, I've simply been able to mold the dog into a workable cottontail hunter. This means that during the course of persuading him to chase rabbits, I slowly ingrain in him the knowledge and understanding that I'm the boss. He can trail and hunt all he wants, but he's going to do it how and when I want it done. He'll also understand that when I'm finished hunting and it's time to go to the truck . . . it's time to go to the truck!

Each dog is an individual, and each learns at a different pace in direct relation to how much time the trainer is willing to devote to the dog. My dogs are notorious for being slow starters, but it's my fault. I always have too many dogs to give any one the individual attention he or she deserves. The dogs always come around, but will almost never hunt their first season. On the other hand, I've sold pups and the new owners had them looking like veterans the first fall. Since they have only one pup, their interest and training are focused on this one individual and it shows. So, the first thing to keep in mind is, the more time and effort you are willing to put into the pup, the more you are likely to get out of it.

Training should begin almost the moment you lay eyes on your new hunting partner. Yes, he should be considered your partner, not just a workhorse so that you don't have to get in the brush. You're going to be a team; anything less and I'll guarantee you'll never get out of the dog what he's capable of. As we mentioned in the chapter on breeding, the bond between you and the dog will begin the first time you pick him up. When treated right, the dog can only like you. I cannot stress enough how important this relationship is, and how it will equate to the dog performing for you in the field. The beagle will hunt, that's almost a given, but he'll perform and do things for you simply because he likes you and wants to please. So keep in mind that as you begin the initial training of getting the dog to chase and trail rabbits, you'll also be working on the other simple commands and developing the bond of friendship between the two of you. Be kind and patient, but also be firm. Let the dog know when you're not happy with what he's doing, and praise him when he's done it right. This is the well-known basis for all training, but it's amazing how many fail to follow this simple advice.

Laying Scent

When the pup is young—say, three months—he won't be up to traipsing into heavy brush to roust a cottontail, but he'll be playful and inquisitive. You can take advantage of this developing curiosity by getting the pup to follow certain scent trails. One of the first things you will notice is that the pup will learn "your" smell quickly and can actually trail you at a very young age. This helps the dog maintain contact with you once you're ready to go to the briar patch. Playing with the pup for a few minutes, then having someone else release him after you've walked away can reinforce this behavior. Stay out of sight, even if only a short distance away, until he finds you, then praise him for the job he's done. Make the game more and more complicated as he gets older, and reward him with treats and praise each time.

I witnessed a vivid example of a hound trailing an owner in 1973 when I worked in a plumbing shop in Uniontown, Pennsylvania. One of the plumbers in the shop was an avid beagler and had a few champion hounds. One morning, just an hour or so after we had begun work, his wife called to say his prized male beagle had escaped from the pen and that they had been looking for him for an hour with no luck. Gerald was beside himself, and quickly informed the boss he'd have to go home and look for his dog.

One of the other fellows had just come inside and heard the commotion.

"That's funny", he said. "I just saw a nice looking beagle outside in the alley."

You guessed it. Gerald's male beagle was standing at the back door next to Gerald's Ford Bronco!

You may say, "So what!" until you know the rest of the details. Gerald lived about three miles on the other side of the fairly large city. The dog had nothing but miles of concrete and paved roads between him and his master. The plumbing shop was situated off a side street totally out of the way of any direct route back to the kennel, and it would have been the wildest stretch of luck to say the dog just happened on that particular alley. It was clear to Gerald, and to the rest of us who saw it, that the dog had simply trailed the Bronco across the city. There was no other explanation.

Getting pups interested in trailing can also be accomplished by laying down other scents: scraps of meat, chicken skin, and old socks saturated with liquid rabbit scent. Tie the material to a string and carefully make a line for the pup to follow. As before, make the game harder each time, but this time the pups gets a reward: the actual item he was trailing, or in the case of the sock, a substitute meaty snack. Of course, you will be contaminating the trail with your own scent, but the pup knows one scent from another. You can also tie the "bait" on a fishing line and cast it some distance, laying scent on the way in, and keeping most of your scent out of the picture.

Quick turns simulate checks, and gaps in the trail may mean "the rabbit" jumped or hopped over something. These early scent trails are fun for the puppy and give the trainer an opportunity to evaluate a dog up close. As the hound gets very good at following the laid meat scent trails, introduce him to the rabbit-scented sock and he will soon be ready to graduate to real live bunnies.

Getting Him Interested in Rabbits

To get the pup interested in rabbits, he must see rabbits. Very few dogs I've owned started only by smelling scent; the dog must see rabbits, at least for a short time. This means that unless you live in an area really buried in rabbits, you've got to rely on other methods. The easiest is to buy or secure several tame rabbits and let the new pup harass them and get a good whiff of scent. I'm sure some will be asking, "Don't tame rabbits smell different from wild ones?" The answer is probably yes, but your dog won't care. Believe me, the dog won't care! For the past twenty years or so, I've had a fenced-in training area in my backyard. In this area there may be a few wild rabbits and several tame ones. In training sessions the dogs pay no attention to what type of rabbit they are running and bark equally well on either type. In my second rabbit video, *Cottontails & Hares*, I devote several minutes to this, actually showing several dogs barking and freely running tame rabbits.

The best domesticated rabbit for training is the San Juan variety, a brown rabbit resembling the wild cottontail, and any other rabbit that is about half grown and is a little "spooky," not having been handled very much. Stay away from any

Puppies can be introduced to tame rabbits when they are about the same size. The dog won't care if he's chasing a tame rabbit and the practice won't ruin the dog in any way.

white rabbits or the floppy-eared varieties, as they are just too tame and will be killed very quickly by the dogs.

A good method to get a pup interested is to place a rabbit on the ground, tethered with a small cord to keep it from running off. Place the pup on a long leash and let him smell and harass the bunny, always keeping the dog just out of reach so he does not injure the rabbit. Some pups will become very aggressive, and some will begin to bark and squeal in their frustration to reach the bunny. A few times of this and the pup will sight chase, if nothing else, the next time he sees a bunny.

There are many variations to this, and these are limited only by your imagination. Some place the pup in a garage or building where some type of maze has been constructed: old cardboard boxes, wheelbarrows, anything to impede the pup's progress and make him search for the bunny. A small temporary wire enclosure can also be staked out in the backyard around trees and shrubs. The theory in any of these training methods is very simple: Once the puppy loses track of the rabbit by sight, it is only natural he'll begin to use his nose to locate this living toy, and he will. Domesticated rabbits are a tremendous help in getting the new pup interested in rabbits and they should not be overlooked. And, they won't ruin a dog, trust me!

Taking a pup for walks in areas where you will encounter rabbits is another good way to encourage him to hunt. Take evening walks, for example, and you will usually see bunnies out feeding along overgrown fields and paths. Once the pup sees a few bunnies and they dart back into the underbrush, he'll naturally begin to put his nose down and begin to smell the scent they leave behind. Encourage him to sniff and hunt, but he'll have to learn much of it on his own. Your job now is to be there when he runs into something unexpected, enforce the rules and commands you are teaching him, and spend as much time as possible with him. The more time you put in with the dog, the quicker he will learn and the better it will be in the long run for you.

You also may want to build a training pen for yourself, or join a beagle club in the area where the dog will encounter rabbits more easily. A training pen requires some space, money, and a good deal of effort to construct it. It is an excellent way to introduce pups to bunnies, but I'd recommend it only to those who are very serious about dog training, and expect to train many dogs in the years ahead.

Beagle clubs offer the advantages of a fenced enclosure, but almost all will require you to spend some time repairing and working at the club, and helping out when the club has a trial or some other function. I consider a training pen and the running grounds of a beagle club as only "introductory" means of getting a pup started on rabbits. These fenced areas rarely simulate actual hunting conditions; plus, both the dogs and the rabbits therein become educated as to what's going on. If the club or enclosure is small with manicured trails, some dogs will become "path hunters." If they are run under such conditions for very long, some will be of little use when asked to perform on real hunts. Good and great dogs, in my opinion, have been hunted and gunned over first, before they became field-trial stars. So, no matter what method you use to get your dog interested in trailing rabbits, get him out hunting as soon as you can, providing he's ready to follow along with you or other hounds.

Follow The Leader

We've all heard about it: Throw the pups in behind the older, experienced dogs and they eventually get trained. This method works, but only to a certain extent. First, the dog that is going to mentor the pup must have very few faults to begin with. If the 'teaching' dog is prone to backtracking or some other major discrepancy in his personality, never, never let the new pup run with him.

Pups will also not have the stamina or the confidence to keep up with older, hard-driving dogs. Within an hour or two the pup, not exactly sure what's going on here, gets bored and tired, and will usually give up the chase and come looking for you. Most of us know what it's like to be on stand waiting for the rabbit and have an antsy pup wandering around 20 yards in front of you. You get frustrated and so does the puppy.

If you are trying to train your pup by running with an older dog, it will certainly have to be done in stages and short stints afield. This is one time when any type of large training pen can be helpful, as the pup can be watched closely and picked up when he begins to fall away from the other dog or simply gets tired of the whole game.

As the pup matures, and his interest in the other dogs (in my case, a small pack) and what they are doing increases, his desire to stay with them becomes stronger than the desire to come see where you are. In general this usually occurs when the dog is ten months to one year old. But this doesn't mean that the dog should be sitting around for the first year; it just means that his training sessions should be short and his runs with the older dogs kept brief enough so that he doesn't get bored and tired. The dog should enjoy his excursions to the field and be excited when he knows he's going out with the bigger boys.

If you plan to run the dog primarily by himself, then he will have to be weaned from his teacher/trainer as soon as possible. Let's say you're out hunting and all of a sudden the dogs are separated and your new trainee is the one that discovers the rabbit. If possible, pick up the older dog, or leash him temporarily, and let the pup try it on his own. If the pup begins to have trouble, unleash the older dog, or walk in and show him the trail the rabbit took, if you know it, and praise him for his good work so far. After all, jumping the rabbit is a big part of rabbit hunting, so you should let the dog know he's done something right. Most dogs will then join in running the rabbit with the other dog; if he doesn't after several such instances, you may have a loner on your hands, and the dog will most likely have to be trained on his own. In any case, give the dog a fair chance to run the rabbit and several attempts at going it alone.

Let's never forget that while your primary goal is to get the new hound to trail rabbits, every trip afield is also a learning experience for him. Don't overload him with everything at once, but if he's not interested in rabbits at the moment, work on showing him how to get through a fence, make a game out of getting across a creek, or practice simple commands such as "No," "Come." "Down!"

If I'm hunting and happen to kill a couple of rabbits, I give the new pup lots of attention and let him mouth the rabbit (without tearing it up) all he wants. If he was with the pack when the bunny was killed, I make it appear as if he was totally responsible for the kill, or at least had a big part in it. I praise him as if he had just done something truly remarkable, even if he was just following along with the pack and not even barking. I do this because I know that next time he'll try a little harder. Slowly the dog will learn many aspects of hunting and hopefully develop into a good gundog. Don't kid yourself: It's not going to be easy and it's not likely to happen overnight, but it will happen.

As I've said before, dogs are individuals and each one must be treated differently. Some train very easily, while some take much more time than you are willing to give. Many dogs will be trained by a combination of methods, and there is nothing wrong with this. So each dog must be judged separately, and you're going to have to evaluate your own dog. Has he seen enough rabbits that you feel he's ready to start trailing? Has he run in the beagle club long enough that he's ready for something else? Is he developing a "me too" attitude from running behind the older pack too much, and is doing little work on his own? I wish I could answer these questions for you, but I can't, as I've never seen your dog. You'll have to do it. Look at the dog closely, be honest, and the answers will come to you.

Proper Gun Dog Behavior

Just because he's a hunting machine, that shouldn't excuse him from not knowing proper hunting etiquette. I've hunted with fellows who had little control over their dogs once they hit the ground. You hunted with the dog, not the reverse. If you wanted to check out particularly nice-looking cover on the next hill and the dog wasn't going that way, too bad. Not me. My theory is: I'm the hunter, he's the dog: I'm the boss. Period!

I think the dog should go easily to the truck without having to be leashed. Once down and hunting, the dog should always be looking for you, noting your location, and changing direction at your command. He should hunt for you, close in if necessary, and not fight with any unfamiliar dogs you might have along on the hunt. When a rabbit is killed, the dog should happily receive praise, and take an interest in the dead bunny, but never try to tear it up, carry it off, or fight over it. When the hunt is over, the dog should understand this and be willing to return to the truck without having to be chased down. All this constitutes good hunting dog etiquette. My dogs all behave this way . . . or they are not my dogs for very long.

So how do we get our dog to act as a "gentleman" in the field? As we said at the beginning of this chapter, training is nothing more than repetition. This means that the dog is leashed and led to the truck every single time he's taken out of the kennel. After awhile, he knows why he's going there, and in time he'll go there readily by himself the moment he's turned loose. Once the leash is no longer needed, verbal commands said to him over and over again while leashed reinforce the training and let him know he's doing right or wrong. A dog with any intelligence at all will learn the trip to the truck is only a prelude to his favorite good time—hunting—and he'll be glad to go there. As with all learned behavior, this may take a great deal of time and will varying greatly between dogs.

Strive to teach the dog 'good hunting etiquette.' When it's time to go to the truck . . . it's time to go to the truck. All my dogs behave this way or they are not my dogs for very long.

The amount of subdued force needed to persuade the dog to listen and learn will again depend on the individual dog. Some learn and behave so well that little formal training is required, while some are truly hardheaded. In fact, a tender subject to many trainers and dog owners is how much force is required. I contend that "to spare the switch is to spoil the dog." The dog must know you're the boss, and crafty dogs will test you to the limits. I don't beat my dogs within an inch of their lives, but, using a small switch or a leather leash across the backside when they are being knot heads does wonders when the dog is misbehaving.

Of course, anytime you discipline a dog in this manner, you must learn to be in total control of yourself. It doesn't take anything more than a firm slap on the buttocks to get a dog back under control. Beating a dog is unnecessary and is not part of a proper training regiment. When a dog does disobey, however, the time to act is the instant the dog gets out of line. I'm tough but fair and humane, but I never let them get away with behavior I won't tolerate. Experience has taught me, that most dogs, after a very short time, will dislike the corrections and the displeasure you show at their negative behavior, that a "mock spanking" becomes as effective as the real thing.

Let's say one of my dogs runs off and goes to visit a dog chained in a yard near where I'm hunting. I may pick up a small branch, get the dog's attention, and when the dog finally returns to me, I may lightly switch it once not really inflicting any real pain–but enough to get the dog to understand that such negative behavior won't be tolerated without correction.

When hunting, I also like to be in control of the dogs at all times. If possible, when a rabbit is killed, I want to be there waiting when the dogs arrive. This way, I can stop any disputes between them with a deep vocal reprimand and, if necessary, a sharp smack on the buttocks of the offender or offenders. Again, I'm not intending to inflict any real pain, but I want the dog to know how it should behave in all situations. If you do nothing in times like this, the dog will become uncontrollable. Little by little with your persistence and guidance, your dog will become a perfect gentleman in the field. If you have developed a good friendly rapport with your hound, most of this simple training will be easy for you and will require little effort on your part. If the dog listens to you in the yard at home, he'll listen to you while hunting. The dog just needs to learn what is expected of him. Each aspect of the hunt it taught as it comes up, and with the same repetitive methods.

Let's say your dog is hunting well with you, following your instructions fairly well, but absolutely abhors going into the truck after the hunt. This is a common problem. How do you handle it? Well, on the day you need to get the animal back in the vehicle, there is little you can do besides the normal coaxing and finally running after the dog, if possible. I've also left dogs in the woods, taken the other dogs home, and came back for them an hour or two later. By then, they are usually very happy to see me.

In a severe case, I went home, picked up my Alaskan Husky, and literally ran the beagle down with this dog! I may add, proudly, that this female beagle, a very tough case for awhile, later became a well-behaved lady and cherished member of my pack. At the time, she was young and still unsure of everything that was going on around her.

Once you have the dog in hand, smack it across the snout with your open hand, or use the switch on it. Be careful here. The dog must know this behavior will not be tolerated, but scolding or beating the dog when it is already frightened will do little to solve any problem.

The author likes to talk to the dog directly to either scold or praise. Don't think for a minute that the dog doesn't know it's being punished.

Use common sense and good judgment. Things are progressing when it takes less persuading and less time to get the dog caged at the end of each hunt. If the dog gives me a particularly bad time, I may also punish it by leaving it home by itself the next day or two. Don't think for a minute the dog doesn't know it's being punished . . . and tell it so!

Also investigate the cause of the problem. In the case where the dog will not go back to the truck, there could be several reasons why he doesn't want to. In many cases the dog simply isn't getting out enough. He knows that when he goes back, he's going to be penned up for a long while again. Fix this by finding some way to get the dog out more, even if someone else must do it. Another reason is the dog simply has a lot of energy and is just not ready to quit hunting. You can understand this, and again you must try to get the dog out for longer stints, but this can only be tolerated to a certain extent. He may be afraid of the dog he's riding with, or some small problem like this. Investigate and find out why he is reluctant to go back to the vehicle. In the end, however, you're still the boss, and when it's time to go—it's time to go.

The beagle may also not want to go to the truck because he gets carsick. Almost all beagles will get used to riding after a time, and this is another item that must be worked on. At first, try short trips to the hunting grounds, say 15 minutes or less. Gradually build up to longer rides as the pup gets used to it. After a few trips and good experiences afield, the pup will begin to turn his attention to what's coming and not to the trip itself. Riding with an older, mellow dog will also help calm an excited youngster.

Another good way to help the young pup overcome carsickness is to cover the cage so he can't see the trees and objects whizzing by. Also turn the crate across the axles, instead of parallel with the truck or car wheels, as this seems to help with some of the motion, and again will help calm him down. As the hound learns to ride and begins to lose his fear of the vehicle, he's less likely to fight the return to the cage. Teaching the pup to ride and return to the cage is another learned behavior, and must be taught the same as every other aspect of hunting. If you can't get the dog to the hunt, or can't get a hold of him when the hunt is over, he's not much good to you.

Running Deer

At some point in the new pup's training, he may begin to run something other than what he was bred for, or what you had intended him to hunt. In most cases, the deer is the single biggest problem for the beagle-equipped rabbit hunter.

Deer are adaptable creatures and will live so close to humans that it is almost unbelievable. Several years ago, at the end of the Pennsylvania's rabbit season, I entered a small thicket that ran right to the edge of a four-lane expressway. The thicket was barely 200 yards wide, and was bordered on the sides by several houses (all relatives of mine). I jumped seven rabbits in the thicket, but counted 20 fresh deer beds! In fact, some of the beds were even pressed right up against the chain-link fence that was supposed to keep deer, kids, and other animals off the road.

Every thicket is home to at least a few deer, and my dogs jump deer accidentally almost every day. It is my opinion (no facts are actually available) that there are now more deer in Pennsylvania than there are rabbits. Since most of us are also deer hunters, it may interest readers to know that buck hunters in the Keystone State killed 203,221 antlered deer in the 2000 season, and new record harvests have been set for several years running. Pennsylvania hunters also kill about 301,379 other, or antlerless, deer during the fall season. Out of these figures archers alone killed 78,522. That's an annual Pennsylvania deer kill of 504,600 animals. (It has also been estimated that 100,000 more deer are killed each year on the highways!)

The author teaches the dogs to walk up a plank so they can load themselves. You can teach a dog almost anything if you are willing to spend the time at it.

Of course, Pennsylvania is not unique to this problem. Almost every state in the Union is seeing a dramatic increase in deer numbers. In a recent article in Reader's Digest, unrelated to hunting, it was noted that nuisance deer are becoming a real problem in state parks. The article also covered the fact that there has been a dramatic rise in deer-automobile collisions. Although human fatalities are rare, the property damage is in the millions of dollars each year. The article stated that 500,000 deer were killed last year on the nation's highways (a very conservative estimate, I would guess). With all these deer, and the fact that our beagles now see them in very close quarters, it is a tremendous temptation for a dog that may have the "deer-running" gene buried deep in his background. This is certainly an enormous temptation to a new pup that's not quite sure what he's supposed to be running anyway.

There is no question in my mind that downright bad behavior in a dog, such as deer chasing, is curable. The problem is that many dog owners don't diagnose the problem quickly enough, and then don't deal with it in a sensible manner. Caught quickly, I believe that deer running and many other problems can be nipped early on with some stern, sometimes hard-hearted action on the owner/trainer's part. Dogs are like children that never grow up. They know exactly what they are supposed to do and what they are not, but they will do exactly as much as they can get away with!

The new dog owner and prospective trainer must face the fact early on that his (perfect) dog may be running a deer. Look for tracks, look for deer, and evaluate the run and the time the dog was away from you. Inspect any and every clue that will help you decide. You do not have to be Einstein to know that the dog is running something other than a rabbit. Face the fact quickly and take actions to stop it immediately. Once the dog gets away with this activity a few times, he is on his way to becoming a full-blown deer runner, and there will be a time when he reaches the point of no return. In this case, his value as a rabbit dog is no longer open for discussion.

In the beginning, if you can get in front of the dog and catch him, a very stern scolding, and/or a mild slap with a leash or small switch is certainly in order. It sounds cruel, and it is, but you can make it as tough as it needs to be. Keep your temper under control and constantly tell the dog what it's being punished for. The point is: Do something! To let the dog get away with this behavior is only asking for trouble later on. I would not hesitate to say that 85 percent of the time the mild beatings and/or good scoldings will break a dog a year or less in age from running deer. It may take a while and several months of patience-trying incidents, but the dog can be broken or taught that he's not to chase this overgrown rabbit.

Of course, there are variables to everything, and along with anything else you may do or try, the dog must be handled carefully when he's a recovering deer addict. First of all, never run him with others that have also been known to run deer. It's true that one bad apple can indeed spoil the whole bunch, and two dogs that are misbehaving are only twice as bad together. Deer runners will pull other dogs along with them even though the other dogs may never run deer on their own. My dog Ralphie never gave a deer track a second sniff, and I've seen him look at deer 25 feet in front of him and never chase them. But I've also seen him "go along for the ride" when he's been with dogs that do run deer. He'll never bark and will be at the end of the pack, but he'll go along just the same.

This is another good tactic in helping you decide if your dog is running deer. If you know of a dog that is virtually 100 percent against chasing deer, he can be used as a "check dog" for others. I've used Ralphie for this many times. If a chase begins and Ralphie doesn't open his mouth within a few minutes, I'm already suspicious. If the chase continues, Ralphie, in most cases, will abandon the line and come back. There is little doubt then that the other dog or dogs are running a deer. Ralphie is a heavy dog, and a little lazy, but he loves to chase rabbits and he is smart enough not to expend a lot of energy on a worthless trail.

One of the main reasons a dog begins to run deer is simple frustration. This occurs when the dogs are in an area where there are few rabbits and the hunting is tough and boring. They've hunted for an hour, or even two, and have failed to jump any rabbits. Suddenly this big brown thing jumps up in front of them and the scent is so strong that you and I can smell it. The strong musky smell rushes up their nose and the temptation to run after it is almost irresistible. One dog squeals, another may bark and sight chase for a short distance, and soon the whole pack is off and running. The chase is on although no one dog is actually a deer runner.

There is not a lot you can do about these situations, and they are common in my area, where we just do not have an enormous population of cottontails. Keep rabbits in front of the dog and the deer chase scenario usually takes care of itself. If possible I try to keep problem dogs out of areas where I know the rabbits are scarce, and I also keep the same dogs out of areas where I'm positive I'm going to jump some deer. It's a tough situation to judge, and I'm constantly juggling dogs on hunts as the season progresses. Of course, I have the luxury of having eight or ten dogs, while most hunters have one or two. If one of their dogs begins chasing deer, they have a real problem on their hands.

Another technique that has had some success is exposing the dog to deer and deer scent early on, under controlled conditions. This is done in a pen or fenced area. The dog can be punished in several ways, or shocked, if he begins to chase or harass the deer. Deer scent sold for archery hunting can be applied to the dog's pen or collar in such a way as to make the dog sick or so familiar with the scent that he has little interest in it. Both of these techniques work for some dogs and are always worth a try.

In the past five to seven years, since I've gotten older, fatter, and a whole lot slower, I have begun to use electronic training collars, commonly called 'shock collars.' I can no longer run down a frisky pup or head off a potential deer chase. What is my opinion of these electronic collars? In the right hands, they can be one of the most effective tools for training a dog. They can be used not just for deer running, but for every aspect of training, such as coming back to the truck after a rabbit hunt or learning a new skill.

An in-depth study of shock collars and their use is not the purpose of this chapter, but some mention must be made of the fact that in the wrong hands, a shock collar is nothing more than torture for the dog. Shocking the dog just to see if it's working or shocking the dog for every little infraction only confuses him. (If you want to see if it's working, grab hold of the electrodes and press the button.) Using the collar just because you're terribly upset with the dog's performance will do little to advance your training efforts. Soon the dog will not understand what he was being admonished for. If you cannot control your temper and have little patience with the dogs now, by all means don't buy a shock collar.

The beagle's short fur and thin, loose skin makes him an ideal candidate for a shock collar. Be careful when using an electric collar. The device will deliver enough of a jolt to this small animal, so again, use caution. If you've decided that a shock collar is the last resort before the dog finds employment elsewhere, by all means use it. The dog, however, needs to be caught in the act, either sight chasing deer or pursuing a hot trail. Be sure. Usually one quick jolt will knock the dog down, and he will be unlikely to take up the trail again at that time. However, a dog that has his mind set on deer will rarely stop after just one shocking, so be ready in the next few trips afield, with collar in place.

A shock collar can be a very effective tool for correcting bad behavior like deer running. Use it with caution. Most collars will give quite a jolt to the short-furred beagle.

Although I will not fool around with or keep a deer runner for very long, I have been able to break some real deer criminals with an electronic collar, and I now have a lot of experience with them. As I have said throughout this book, every dog is different and has his own personality. Some are poor candidates for shock collars, and will simply run into the next county when correction is applied. I have also found, however, that most of these dogs are poor candidates for any type of correction and learning. But, in general, electronic training collars are so valuable that I am seldom on a hunt where two or three of my dogs aren't wearing one. They give you that peace of mind that you have the dog under control, and if some type of emergency comes up you can get the dogs back on the truck quickly or even save a dog's life. They are that useful.

The point is, the shock collar is a valuable instrument for the dog trainer who is competent enough to use it safely and humanely.

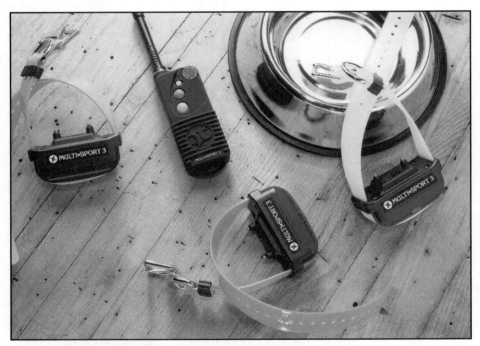

An electronic collar is a valuable instrument for the dog trainer who is competent enough to use it wisely. Pictured is a Tri-Tronics Multi-Sport 3—a dog trainer can control three dogs from a single transmitter at one-half mile range.

The Training's Never Over

During this chapter on training I've been repetitive on some things on purpose, and I state again that most training is nothing more than repetition. This means that almost anyone with a little common sense and more than a little patience can train a dog. Again, what you expect from the dog will surely not happen overnight, but it will happen. The amount of effort put forth by both you and your dog during the early period of training will be the determining factor in how great the dog becomes in the years ahead. Keep in mind that the dog doesn't have to be a polished veteran when training season is over and it's time to go hunting. Much of what a dog learns and knows will be taught on the job, as he takes part in the hunt.

I've never taken much stock in the adage, "You can't teach an old dog new tricks." The truth is that you can teach a dog, old or young, just about anything if you're willing to spend the time at it. Remember, it's just repetition . . . repetition . . . repetition.

A pack of four or five dogs brings a whole new dimension to the game of beagling. Once you experience the thrill, noise and excitement this brings to the chase, it is difficult to go back to running one dog again!

9

BUILDING A HUNTING PACK

Being a die-hard rabbit hunter, I hunt in any weather. Here in Pennsylvania, the season is so short that you would do very little hunting if you waited for perfect days. Also, I've sometimes expanded my hunting into other states simply to extend hunting time. When you arrive somewhere hundreds of miles from home, you're going to hunt no matter what the weather. And depending on one single dog never seemed like a great idea to me . . . especially when I've just driven 500 miles to hunt rabbits!

Each dog is an individual. Some have great noses. Others are exceptional jump dogs, uncannily knowing where every cottontail is hiding. Still others are noted for having untiring energy, replacing little talent with sheer determination and desire.

Mix all these factors together, blend in dry, hot conditions or hard, frozen ground, and it becomes apparent that one dog can't do it all. One day, I came up with the conclusion that if one dog was having a tough time, another could only help . . . and then, if the two were struggling, three would certainly be better. Of course, this is a hollow conclusion and only a hope or wish at best. Even though I routinely run several dogs at a time, I still believe that one and maybe two dogs, that can hunt independently and circle their own bunnies, are definitely the more valuable commodity and the best choice for the beginning beagler. But, I enjoy the additional noise and action that extra dogs bring to the hunt, and my small pack has slowly evolved. At one time, there were almost no pack hunters in my area, so I was breaking new ground here, and I got some strange looks and comments when I encountered others hunters with my pack in tow. I now rarely hunt with fewer than four or five dogs. In the various dog organizations and at most trials, a small pack is usually anything from three to ten dogs. A large pack is anything over ten dogs.

For those who don't normally run a "pack," it is sometimes difficult to find and develop dogs that are of similar speed or temperament to run together. Each dog has to have some independence, but must be smart enough and mellow enough to realize he's part of a team effort. If the dog has any brains at all, he'll simply adjust his speed one way or the other, readily help out at the checks, or go to the dog that has located the trail. There will almost always be a lead dog, but he will not "horse" the trail so much that he pulls away from the rest, or is afraid to accept help from the second dog or any of the others. He has to be a team member too.

Under ideal conditions, a pack operates as a single unit. A well-matched pack is especially beautiful to listen to, a thing of beauty, and truly a sight to behold. As any old houndsman will tell you, it's nothing less than music.

The main drawback to hunting with a pack is that the dogs begin to rely on each other to get the job done. No one dog is taxed unduly, but every dog is dependent on the others. Many times, the greatest dog in the pack is lost when hunting on his own. In reality, it would be much better if a dog would be trained on his own first, learning to hunt and jump his own rabbit, learning to circle the rabbit totally on his own, and then be introduced to the pack.

Of course, there's a problem with this theory as well. Some dogs trained on their own, outside of a pack, simply will not run with any other dogs, or are so independent that they won't adjust their speed, let the others help them, or adapt to any other behavior crucial to the success of the pack and, consequently, the success of the chase and ultimately the hunt. Some dogs are also natural loners, and will never fit into a pack, period.

Pack pups are trained rather easily. They are put down with the normal lead dogs and a natural game of "follow the leader" ensues. Pups trained this way take longer to open up on rabbits, but will develop their own running style (within the pack), bark, searching ability, and so on. Yes, all the dogs in the pack soon learn that the game doesn't begin until someone finds a rabbit, so they all search (some much better than others). During these early outings, the pups receive a lot of on-the-job training: they are leashed to and from the truck, learn to ride, are shown plenty of dead rabbits, and are generally exposed to the procedures of hunting.

I don't expect a new pup to do much the first season except follow the other dogs. If he does that much, he will learn, even if slowly, everything he'll need to run within the pack. Some pups take to the whole thing quickly, are interested in everything that goes on, and are excited when the rabbit is killed. Others take longer, and some never quite become the pack dog that you hoped they would.

I should mention that in a lot of cases, pups that develop slowly sometimes turn out to be very good dogs, so give each dog a chance. Unless I get totally frustrated with a certain hound I'll allow him (mostly her) to stay around for two complete hunting seasons. By then the dog has had plenty chances to perform. Even while running five or six dogs, it is easy to observe, listen, and judge who is doing what and which one is doing little more than following along barking. Remember, the pack is a closely knit team; every member must do some of the work. No matter how pretty the dog is, or how much I like the dog, I cannot justify keeping and feeding a beagle that is a mediocre performer. I usually give such dogs away, and most people make great pets out of them.

There are many aspects about building or hunting with a small pack, but one aspect I'd like to mention in particular is that in most cases a pack is built gradually, often over the course

One day I decided that if one dog was having a tough time another could only help, and the idea of building a small pack slowly evolved. I enjoyed the noise and excitement additional dogs brought to the hunt. Here, Bill Morgan shows cottontails to a pair of young Swiss Hounds just learning how to hunt as a team; later, they would become members of a larger pack.

of years. The pack will consist of dogs of different ages, which means some members will have to be replaced from time to time. Some dogs will also develop bad habits, or will simply not do enough to justify their membership in the pack. These dogs must be also culled from the pack, and replaced with new pups. Do such culling carefully, as sometimes dogs are sold or lost and the pack suffers much more than you had expected.

I built my pack slowly, beginning with my first dog, Berries. She was an aggressive, fast dog—not an exceptional trailer, but a remarkable jump dog and great hunter. Over a five- to ten-year period, I threw many dogs in behind her. Most she simply outran and didn't care whether they were with her or not. Then, as she grew older, she had a litter of pups that included Buster. Buster was raised with her, and they became close companions. As Buster began running, Berries slowed down some, and they became a great team.

Then, a few years later, along came Buster's daughter, Sue-Sue. Like Berries, Sue-Sue was a great jump dog and hunter, but lacked the good nose I had hoped she would have. The three dogs complemented each other beautifully, however. If one lost the trail, all searched for it. Together Sue-Sue and Berries rousted every bunny in the country. Each ran about the same speed, and they were devastating on the rabbit population. As Berries became too old to run and Buster and Sue-Sue took on more responsibility of leading the pack, I began breeding my own dogs to acquire these same qualities and to get dogs that, because they were from the same family, ran at roughly the same speed. By then, it was pretty clear that I would never go back to running a single dog.

As you can see, keeping a good pack together is a tough and sometimes frustrating chore. Over the years scores of dogs have "auditioned" for my pack; few have become established members. But, and I can't say it enough, seeing a well-oiled pack working together as a single machine is one of the greatest experiences of rabbit hunting.

Berries was my first real hunting dog and later the foundation of my venture into pack hunting. Although not an exceptional trialer, she was a great, aggressive hunter and became even better when other dogs were along to give her a hand. Hunted mostly by herself, she later became very accustomed to running in a small pack.

10

IN DAYS GONE BY

A s we're rabbit hunting, we stumble onto places and things that reek of history and sometimes, in some places, you can almost hear voices crying out from days gone by. So it was that I stumbled onto a spot early in 1996 that is by far one of the neatest places I have ever hunted.

A friend had invited me in there, and she said, "I'm sure there's rabbits in there around all those old buildings and stuff. That used to be quite a bustling place when the coke ovens were working."

So one Saturday, my buddy Bob Clarke and I walked the dogs into this strange museum of old buildings, slag piles, and coke ovens. It is called Briar Hill, interesting enough, and is only about 15 miles from my home.

Vines, various weeds, and now trees dug into the sides of all the structures. Stone-arched windows and massive doorways graced the various houses and coal company buildings. Corner stones dating back to the 1700s made the place downright eerie.

"Boy, what a place, huh?" I say to Bob. "This must have been some place at one time." To the West, beyond the main complex, stretched rows and rows of coke ovens, their flames and connection to the steel mills in Pittsburgh extinguished nearly 40 years before.

Bob kicked up the first rabbit, then shot him quickly after the dogs made a small circle. I mentioned something about the rabbit never having been chased by a dog before.

Annie kicked up the next one, so I moved up into the main group of buildings. The rabbit was heading East on the far side of a long, exceptionally large, stone building. All the windows were gone, and there was graffiti sprayed on the south wall. I shook my head, and turned my attention back to the chase. The dogs were still working East, and I saw that Bob had moved in on that end of the building, I expected him to shoot at any moment.

The chase was heating up, and the dogs sounded muffled, their voices echoing and bouncing off the buildings everywhere. Bob didn't shoot, and I could tell the dogs had turned away from him . . . and that's when I realized they were coming right down the center of the building!

Vines, various weeds and even trees fight to destroy the old buildings, slag piles and coke ovens of Briar Hill.

I was in some sort of trance as the giant cottontail came bounding out the center door right in front of me! He caught me by surprise on the first shot, and I knew he was just too close for the pattern. He kept going, and the second shot found its mark, tumbling the bunny into a nearby rose bush. The dogs gleefully came rushing out the door, and joined in on the celebration. It was a classic run.

"Wow! Did you see that?" I nearly screamed at Bob.

"Yeah, that was something," he replied. "Well, that's home for them. I'll bet there's more around."

Bob and I took two more large rabbits, but an unseasonably warm day forced us to quit early that morning. Yet, we had found a remarkable hunting spot.

"You know," I said, "Tony Rinaldi is coming down in a few weeks. Why don't we bring him over here? He would get a kick out of hunting in here."

"Sounds like a plan," Bob agreed.

So, on the morning of January 24th, 1997, Bob, Tony Rinaldi, and I strolled into the abandoned town of Briar Hill.

Tony was instantly amused at the strange sight.

"Hey look, there's a fire hydrant right here in the woods, and Bowser's peeing on it!" he said, laughing.

We wandered around checking out buildings, looking at old bottles and miscellaneous junk, when Bowser let us know that the first rabbit was up. We zigzagged around several structures to find the dogs heading south near the edge of town. They lost that rabbit, but jumped another while they were trying to pick up the check . . . it came running down an old coal haulway right in front of me . . . and I was "forced" to shoot it. It was a nice bunny.

As I'm cleaned that one, the dogs jumped another and began running it around buildings in the main complex. I was still working on my rabbit when it began to sleet, then rain, and I knew we were in for a tough, wet day if it didn't let up.

The dogs holed their rabbit at the rear of a smaller stone building, and I stopped there long enough to snap a few pictures. We were just about ready to leave the main town, and get into the outskirts where there were plenty more vines and rose bushes, when Annie jumped yet another bunny. It squirted out toward Bob and I let him know, but he didn't shoot, and I could see the bunny slip back onto the trail in front of me.

Annie was screaming and some of the dogs were already in with her as they cut across the path in front of me. I had no plans to shoot the rabbit when I suddenly saw him break left and dive onto an ash dump 45 yards out, broadside to me. I swung with him for a second or two, then couldn't keep myself from squeezing the trigger. The bunny went down in a spectacular cartwheel, and I was instantly greeted by shouts of, "GH!! GH!! GH!," from Bob. Translated, that means "Game Hog," and I knew I better not shoot anymore for a while.

It was raining harder as we moved out of town into the main coke field. It was another eerie sight, and Tony was full of questions. I tried to explain the coke-making process, as we peered into several of the beehive structures. I told him I could remember some of them still working when I was a kid, and Bob was quick to remind us that that was a long time ago! Yet, I can remember a few coke ovens glowing brightly in the night sky, and seeing railroad cars full of the gray-black rocks being pushed into the steel-making towns along the river. That was a long time ago, and now there were hundreds of the brick beehives being taken over by weeds, trees, and being used by uncaring people as sites for their garbage dumping.

The rain continued to come down, and after nearly an hour's lull in the action,

Bowser, Sherri, Annie, and Sammy found another rabbit. It went north up a steep hollow, and with Tony on one side and Bob and me on the other, I figured it would be a short run. I hung back, not wanting to shoot another rabbit when no one else had any.

Bob was in a good spot, about 30 yards in front of me, and the dogs were going straight up the side of the hill right for him. I was waiting for him to shoot, when I looked down into the hollow at the little creek below and here came the rabbit! He leaped across the creek and entered a heavy section of brush on the other side. I glanced at the

The author can remember a few active coke ovens brightly glowing in the night sky and seeing railroad cars full of the gray-black rocks on the way to steel mills in Pittsburgh. The ovens are now slowly crumbling and are a refuge for many cottontails.

dogs that were just reaching the top of the hill, and they started their turn to come back into the hollow. I took a chance the rabbit would sit still for a few minutes and motioned for Bob to get over to my position.

"You see that big cherry tree over there?" I said. "He's in that big clump of brush to the left. The dogs will push him out of there in a minute." Bob nodded his approval, and I stepped back to let him get set.

He barely had time to get ready when the rabbit came bounding out of the brush, and went streaking up the far side of the creek. Bob let fly our special No. 4 late-season load and the bunny tumbled.

"Game Hog, huh? Now I've got to spot and set you up for them!" We both had a good laugh and Tony retrieved the rabbit from his side of the valley.

It was early afternoon, and I was pretty soaked, but agreed to check out another hill that was just loaded with vines and multiflora rose. It was torture in there, but I had only gone 50 yards when I saw a rabbit sneaking uphill away from the dogs. I called the hounds over, and Bowser went tearing away, taking the rest of the pack in tow.

This was a good run, but I was wondering how we would ever kill this rabbit. It was so thick that you couldn't see 20 feet in front of you. Only heavily trodden deer paths broke the rose here and there. Tony was directly below me in the only opening of any significant size. The dogs by then had looped the top of the hill, come in to my left, and turned downhill. I knew the rabbit had to be there somewhere, and I took off my orange hat and waved it around to let Tony know where I was.

When he saw my hat, he yelled, "The rabbit is sitting right in behind you . . . right between me and you!"

The bunny came running by, and I poked the gun into an opening and fired a hopeless shot sideways. I knocked a few bushes down, but that was it. I forced myself back into the opening with Tony.

"It's impossible to see in there," I said. "I'll get behind you, so you can shoot. This is the only good opening around anywhere."

The dogs were having a tough time getting through the roses, but the adrenaline was pumping, and they were slowly pushing him around again. For a few seconds they broke right, and I was thinking I'd see the rabbit again, when they turned back toward the opening. It was a perfect set up, and the rabbit bolted out right in front of Tony. It was his first and only rabbit of the day.

The dogs ran a few more rabbits, but the chases ended quickly at the entrances to ground hog holes, and I knew the incoming bad weather was pushing them in. But we checked out more brush on the way out. On this side of town, only stone foundations mark the spot of a once-bustling community. All the wood of the clapboard-sided houses is now gone. I suspect many were burned by vandals, and in many places only depressions in the ground speak about where once some structure stood.

We worked back into the main part of town, and I got the guys to stop long enough to pose in one of the windows with the dogs. The icy rain was steady now, and I didn't have to work very hard to persuade the guys to go to the truck. The dogs, cold, tired, and wet, were eager to climb into the carpeted boxes.

Tony took one last look around, as I snapped a few parting pictures.

"This must have been one thriving community at one time," he said. "Boy, if only some of these buildings could talk, huh, Dave?"

"Yeeupp, in days gone by I'll bet there were hundreds of people working down in here. And I don't think there were many rabbits shot coming out of the door-ways!"

Back in the main part of town, I get the guys to stop long enough to pose in one of the giant windows for a picture. In days gone by, there were many people living and working here, and not too many rabbits were shot coming out of the doorways!

11

SEEKING THE QUARRY

Why a chapter on searching out cottontails? Well, this book was written mostly for the novice beagler and the rabbit hunter who doesn't have years of experience under his fluorescent-orange hat. Anyone with a little effort can go out and roust a few cottontails and have a fairly successful day. But, how about consistently getting up rabbits and taking them in unknown territory or in bad weather conditions?

Since my dad didn't hunt, I began hunting by myself or with friends from the neighborhood. None of us knew much about it; we just went out, stomped around, and once in awhile killed a few bunnies. At the time, I wish I would have had someone to offer a little advice; hence this chapter on seeking out cottontails.

You've probably heard the old saying, "Only ten percent of the lake holds ninety percent of the fish." This is also appropriate when referring to rabbit hunting. About ten percent of a given area holds ninety percent of the rabbits in that area. Why this anomaly occurs is anyone's guess. You would expect it to be tied directly to the type of cover hunted, but I've seen identical cover hold all kinds of rabbits on one side of a hill, yet not hold any on the other.

Of course, early in the season, rabbits are spread out and can be found just about anywhere, but later, as cover dwindles and rabbits receive some hunting pressure, they back off these thin fringe areas and become more difficult to locate. Large weed fields that held rabbits early on become nothing more than dry wastelands, and nothing more than a waste of time for the hunter and his pack. Here in the northern states, where cold and snow become a factor in late-season rabbit hunting, successful hunters pay close attention to food sources available to the cottontail, as well as to heavy cover nearby. This sounds simple enough, but you'd be surprised how many hunters take little notice of why they found a cottontail in a particular spot.

A friend and I were having a disappointing day hunting cottontails one warm November day. It had been extremely dry for weeks, and we just couldn't locate anything. Then the solution hit me in the face. I came over a steep rise hot and sweating, and just the sight of water, and the cool refreshing breeze from a lake in the next valley, made me feel better.

"That's it!" I told my buddy. "There have to be rabbits around that water, where it is cool and wet." And there were. The dogs ran several and we shot most of them standing on the edge of the lake. In this case the rabbits needed something; it wasn't food, but it was something just as important. It should have been obvious, but it just never occurred to us. It does now, and we've since used this experience to our advantage many times.

Since I am fairly well known around my area as an avid rabbit hunter, I'm often asked to take people out on their first rabbit hunt. In some cases they really only want to use my dogs, but that is another story. I'm not sure I enjoy these hunts very much, as I spend most of my time worrying about whether I, or one of my dogs, am going to be accidentally shot, but it does give me a chance to observe fellows who know almost nothing about the sport.

The first thing a novice rabbit hunter should do is tie a 20-pound lead weight around his leg. It's comical sometimes. We enter a heavy thicket side by side and pretty soon we can't see each other. The dogs jump a rabbit, I yell for my new hunting companion, and he's six acres away already through the thicket and standing in an open field! I burst out laughing, and it puts a damper on the whole day.

Seriously, the first thing a hunter must do if he wants to consistently find bunnies is to slow down. And I mean slow down! A rabbit has very few defenses: one is to run, another is to sit still, and this he does extremely well until you simply walk by him. I witnessed a great example of this just a few weeks ago. A couple of friends and I were hunting an area and the dogs had a rabbit up. During the run, three other guys entered the thicket and came our way. I dispatched the rabbit that the dogs were running, and our party decided to head back to the truck for lunch. We passed by the other three hunters who were quickly walking Army-style out through the brush. Although we covered the same ground they had just walked through, we jumped three more rabbits before we reached the road!

A rabbit is small, almost tiny in comparison to his surroundings. He can hide in unbelievably small amounts of cover. If you can hide a softball in it, a cottontail can hide there. That means a hunter needs to look over every single piece of brush, check out every fallen treetop, and kick every stump and bush in sight. Forget patterns. Have no set routine or speed. Zigzag through the area, stop frequently, and kick everything in sight. This haphazard style will make your quarry very nervous, and he is not likely to sit still for it.

While you're stumbling around looking for this hidden softball, your dogs should also be doing something, hopefully hunting. This gives them time to thoroughly work over the area. Don't expect the dogs to find every rabbit, because they won't, and on many hunts I roust far more than the dogs. Remember you're a team, they do their part when they're needed, but don't expect them to do it all. Yes, I expect them to roust some game and I'm displeased with them (and I let them know it) when I find a rabbit in a clump of brush they've already checked out, but they make up for it many times over. As with yourself, don't rush the dogs. Let them work. On some days I may hunt a ten-acre thicket for several hours, where others would walk through it in 15 minutes.

OK, let's go on a simulated hunt. It is several weeks into the season, a lot of brush is mashed and mangled, and it is a cold 20° F. You've got one partner with you and at least two frisky beagles. If you're lucky, the beagles will find you a rabbit or two, but as I mentioned before, I don't expect them to do everything. The dogs certainly can't look around and judge like I can standing six feet out of the brush. So what do you look for?

Start out by gazing around the entire area and noting areas that are, or at least appear to be, unusually thick, areas that have few if any hunter paths beaten through them. Also hunt the edges along open fields so long as they haven't been smashed and beaten into the ground. The rabbits will use these fields to feed at night, and some will be sitting just off the field about ten to twenty yards in any cover available. When hunting the really thick stuff, make straight entries into the brush while encouraging your dogs to follow you and stick close. Keep penetrating these tangles, getting in as far as you can, then backing out. Find another spot, penetrate again, then back out. In time, you will jump a bunny, or your dogs will pick up the scent and roust him for you. Your partner should stay on the outside in more open terrain, watching for bunnies that may slip out undetected. Take turns and both of you will get some shooting, and hopefully the dogs will get some action by running rabbits that escaped the heavy cover. If hunting alone, you still have to penetrate the brush, but you'll have to rely more on the dogs for your shooting once the cottontail is up and running.

While you're checking out these likely spots, also keep on the lookout for fallen trees. These are probably the most productive areas, as rabbits love to take refuge in the tops of trees, especially after they've been down at least one growing season, and grass and weeds have encased some of the branches. Find a place where someone has been cutting trees for firewood and you'll find cottontails under the tops. Go out of your way to check out these treetops, as it will be worth it. Stay away from places where a bulldozer was used to clear trees and brush; there may be some cottontails there, but the piles will be so tight, and there will be so many holes to hide in, that a hunter can spend a whole day in there and have very little to show for it.

Of course, any veteran cottontail hunter knows that rabbits love ground-growing vines. Rip-shins, multiflora rose, dewberries, and a host of other vines are used by the cottontail for food and cover. His favorite in our part of the world is honeysuckle, in which he sits and eats. It is one of his favorite foods. I have killed so many cottontails from patches of honeysuckle vines that I never leave the woods without checking out every single one I can find-they're that productive.

We're assuming here that you've never hunted this particular area before, and these are the places I would begin my search for cottontails. Sooner or later you'll encounter some, but keep in mind that some areas are simply better for cottontails than others. Since I believe it doesn't take much to feed a cottontail, and they'll eat just about anything, some other factor must be keeping their numbers down in many places. This almost has to be predators, including the winged variety. Domesticated dogs and house cats kill cottontails by the thousands, and I believe that the common house cat is as great a threat to the rabbit population as any wild predator. This type of pressure also turns cottontails into strictly nocturnal animals, making hunting them nearly impossible. In this situation, the hunter should consider hunting the very first hours after daylight, and the last couple hours before dark. Some cottontails will be up and around at this time of the day, and the hunter may be surprised at his success in areas he thought were devoid of rabbits.

Once you've hunted an area, the search for cottontails becomes a little easier, and each time through you gain more and more knowledge of the habitat. In places where I have hunted for years, I know exactly where I'm likely to find bunnies. In these same areas are places where I have yet to find a cottontail, and I avoid them. It saves time, plus wear and tear on the dogs and on me.

As you become familiar with a spot, mentally mark each location where cottontails were rousted, particularly their escape paths should they get away. More than likely you will encounter the rabbit or another in this same place next time, and nine times out of ten he'll run the same way.

Catching Them Sitting

When you begin to consistently catch rabbits "sitting," you are probably turning into a very good rabbit hunter. This means you're starting to get tuned in to the whole hunting experience and that you're really paying attention. I know some pretty fair rabbit hunters who have never found one single rabbit sitting, and this amazes me. It tells me a lot about how serious they are about rabbit hunting.

Rabbits are not hard to spot sitting, and with a little practice it's easy. To illustrate this, I have included a picture of one "dug in" somewhere. So how can I find rabbits sitting? First off, I expect to find rabbits sitting. That simply means I know every rabbit will not bolt at the sound of my approach, so I can expect to see some hiding if I look around carefully. Remember, the rabbit has only a couple of defenses: run, or sit still. In some cases, he will sit still.

When looking for these sitters, you've got to look at the brush much more intensely. Don't just gaze out through the brush. Look at each bush, each individual

Hunters talk about looking for the rabbit's eyeball and how this gives him away when he is sitting. When you can't seem to find an entire rabbit sitting, it will do little good to go around looking for eyeballs! The rabbit's ball-like shape and the distinguishing fur texture will stand out better for someone searching out cottontails. It just takes a little practice and getting "tuned in" to spotting them.

weed, and each small sapling. Don't just look at a small grove of trees; look at each individual tree, studying the base carefully. Expect to see a cottontail dug in at the base of every tree, and I guarantee you will begin to see them.

For years, I heard hunters talk about looking for the rabbit's eyeball and how this gives him away when he is sitting. I guess sometimes it does, but it has rarely worked for me. Remember we said the entire rabbit is barely the size of a softball, especially when curled up in a form, so how big do you think his eyeball is? When you can't find an entire rabbit sitting, it will do little good to go around looking for eyeballs! Instead, concentrate on seeing a rabbit. Look especially for a clump of rabbit fur, and you'll soon discover that the rabbits' round ball-like shape and the distinguishing fur texture stand out better than you ever imagined. The fur will seem reddish brown, sleek, and shiny, especially if the sun is shining on it. Almost every cottontail has some white on him, and a few white hairs mixed in on his back. These tiny white streaks combined with the familiar texture of brown rabbit fur will betray the bunny's hiding place. Pay attention, and you'll be spotting sitting rabbits in no time.

Sometimes weather conditions, rabbits' seasonal habits, the time of day, the type of brush you're hunting in, and other variables can make rabbits seem as if they're an endangered species. They're not. They're still there, but sometimes you have to work a lot harder to find them. Those who can still manage to get a few up and running in unfamiliar terrain, or in bad weather, are the hunters I enjoy hunting with. In most cases, these hunters have been able to learn something from almost every rabbit hunt. They can spot the ten percent of the area where most of the rabbits will be hiding, and they find their share of sitters.

In rabbit hunting, the game doesn't begin until the rabbit is found. That's why they call it hunting. Pay attention. Be aware of your surroundings at all times, and ask, "Why was that rabbit sitting there?" In searching out cottontails, there's no big secret to it; it's still a lot of hard work. Pay attention! (Did you notice that's the third time I've said that? Or was it the fourth?) If you're really paying attention, finding cottontails should get a little easier each time out.

12

WHY THEY CIRCLE
AND WHY THEY HOLE UP

W
hy a rabbit circles, and why he holes up are topics that have been the bases for much discussion and many arguments between rabbit hunters and beagle owners for what seems like eternity. Each topic could be expanded into a chapter, or even an entire book of its own. I don't intend to spend a lot of valuable space and time on either subject, or expect to settle the argument here, as it is impossible to know what's in a rabbit's mind when he suddenly decides to turn the corner, or just as quickly goes to ground. Rabbits circle-that's a fact. They also hole up.

I am convinced, however, that under certain circumstances a rabbit's actions can be fairly predicable. My theories and thoughts concerning both of these inherited bunny traits are derived from spending thousands of hours hunting and studying them. The answer to why a rabbit circles is simpler and easier to understand than why a rabbit holes up, so we'll discuss that trait first. Keep in mind that although I am mainly talking about cottontails, hares and other species also exhibit the same behavior for the same reasons. Although the hare or swamp rabbit may have a larger home territory, he still returns or circles much like a cottontail, it just takes him a little longer.

The Circle Pattern

I may have already given away the answer to why a rabbit circles, and it won't be a surprise to most experienced rabbit hunters. The cottontail and most all his cousins return roughly to the area where they were kicked up because they simply do not wish to leave their home territory.

In articles I have written for various outdoor magazines, I have explained the "circle theory" many times. In my first video on cottontail rabbit hunting, I also went into much detail about it, including showing a cottontail's precise path across a hillside. The key to understanding why a rabbit behaves this way is tied directly to his home territory.

As a child your territory was perhaps the backyard. As you grew it expanded to maybe the neighbor's next door, and finally the entire neighborhood. In this environment (your territory) you felt safe and secure. Only if chased by the neighborhood bully would you dare be pushed out of your familiar turf. It is the same with a rabbit. Each rabbit has his own particular territory that he calls home. This territory is sometimes clearly marked by some natural boundary—a creek, an old fenceline, or maybe just the edge of an open field. The rabbit has probably spent his entire life inside this territory, and is extremely reluctant to leave it.

Brian Salley has found that this large tree marking an old fence line and property boundary is also the edge of a rabbit "territory." Reading the terrain and knowing where the cottontail might show up can be a big advantage when hunting.

When the rabbit reaches one of these imaginary boundaries, even pushed by dogs, he simply turns and runs the edge of his territory, or turns completely around and slips by the dogs. As the dogs continue to push the little critter, he will eventually end up pretty close to where he was first located.

That brings us to another point that should not be overlooked. Many people believe that well-trained dogs actually make the rabbit circle, but this isn't the case. Although we wish we could train dogs to circle the bunny, they have nothing to do with the circle pattern. A good trailing hound simply follows the scent trail no matter where it goes. If he does his job right, and the rabbit begins to circle, he (Old Rover) will end up back at the same place as well.

Of course, there are exceptions to every rule, and once in awhile you will encounter a rabbit that takes off straight away and never looks back. These are just that: exceptions. And even the exceptions can be explained sometimes, especially running rabbits in March. The hunter has encountered a buck rabbit that spent the night wandering around in search of receptive does. When the bunny is rousted in the morning he heads straight back to his home territory. In general, however, most rabbits will make a conscious effort to stick to the area they are most familiar with—and thus they develop circle patterns.

The term "circle" is a little misleading in terms of rabbit hunting. In most cases the rabbit arcs or runs a pattern much like the shape of a balloon on a string, or a large oval. Let's say you've just jumped a rabbit at the end of the string. A normal rabbit run will find the rabbit running straight up the string for some distance. As he begins to pull away from the dogs, he slows down and begins to "arc" and run the circumference of the balloon. When he reaches the imaginary string again, he will turn and often come back down the same trail he went up. This is typical, and I have seen this pattern hundreds of times. It is conceivable that the rabbit does this by smell, and it is a way of keeping his bearings inside his territory. It could also be a way of distracting the dogs, but this is unlikely; in most cases, the rabbit is simply using his nose to backtrack his own footsteps, thus keeping him inside his territory.

When hunting cottontails, I do not nail myself down to the exact spot where the bunny was rousted. If I encounter a situation such as the one just mentioned, I will follow the dogs "up the string" for a little way until I find a good open place for a stand. In areas where I hunt, staying put in heavy brush will net you very few cottontails. They may circle back to within a few feet of where they were sitting, but you'll never get a shot at them.

Also, on some runs or chases, the rabbit pursued by the dogs will soon set up a pattern and pass through certain openings or around certain obstacles several times. This is because during his weeks and months of living in this particular area, the rabbit has marked these boundaries with scent from a gland under his chin. While in the field for reasons other than rabbit hunting, you may have witnessed this behavior of rabbits rubbing their chins on sticks and small trees. Again, if you are out to kill the rabbit, it pays to be a little flexible. If I notice the rabbit starting to run a pattern around these scent markers or obstacles, I quickly move to one of these points. If he has passed through an opening at least twice, I'm there when he attempts it the third time.

So, in most cases, rabbits circle to avoid being pushed out of their neighborhood or territory. And it is a good thing they do, or most of us would kill very few cottontails, and our dogs would be of little use to us. It is apparent, however, that cottontails will adapt and do anything to survive. In areas where they have been pressured by dogs and hunted extensively, their circle patterns have become less pronounced. On the other hand, in the mountainous areas around my home, I find far fewer cottontails, but since most have never been run by dogs before, they stick to their home turf much better, run much truer patterns, and are therefore easier to bag.

Why They Hole Up

Understanding why a rabbit goes into a hole while he is being pursued should be relatively easy, but it isn't. The primary reason that was stated just a few minutes ago is obvious: the rabbit wants to survive. Then why have you seen rabbits pass scores of holes, then suddenly decide to enter one? Well, to understand the rabbits' logic we would have to think like he does, and sort of get inside his head. That is almost impossible, but we can rely on the knowledge at hand, the experience of many hunts, and the actions of hundreds of rabbits. Also, a rabbit may pass several holes and not enter them for the most obvious reason: there is another creature already down there, in some cases a predator that will surely eat him! Remember that the cottontail is not stupid. He lives every minute of his life in the woods. He has a good nose and knows exactly what's hiding in that otherwise great-looking burrow. In a case such as this he'll pass and take his chances with the beagles pursuing somewhere behind him. (Incidentally, rabbits do not dig their own burrows, but use the holes of other creatures.)

Again, I have written about my theories concerning "why they hole up" in many publications over the years, but my opinions have changed little. Keep in mind that you may have formulated some of the same opinions but never realized it, nor stopped to think about it.

Every single rabbit hunt is different, but after awhile a definite pattern to the rabbits' general behavior is noted. A good rabbit hunter learns to evaluate all these different behavior patterns and each situation and files them away to be used later. Sometime, maybe months later, he may say, "Hey, I know what that rabbit will do," and then he goes ahead and does exactly what you predicted. In a sense you have gotten inside the rabbit's head and begun to think ahead of him. Many times it is no accident that we are standing in the exact spot where the rabbit crosses an opening. All of us have done this one time or another, but many of us fail to learn anything from it. But every time a rabbit enters a hole we should learn something from it and at least come up with a reasonable explanation as to why Mr. Cottontail decided to duck out of the picture. We may not be right each time, but remembering the incident, and filing away the information, will make us better rabbit hunters. Following, in order of importance, are the main reasons why rabbits hole up.

Weather. Without a doubt, any change in the weather has a major effect on the cottontails' actions. I'm sure most of us have been on hunts where practically every bunny kicked up went straight to a hole. In many cases, the weather change was obvious, and this situation is common when a storm is moving into the area. We do not know for sure why the rabbit holes up, but it probably goes back to the survival extinct. Again, put yourself in the rabbit's position. Dogs are pursuing him, the air pressure is dropping, and a storm is coming. I would surmise that the rabbit realizes he is in some danger here and, coupled with a storm moving in on him, he does not want to be pushed anywhere he feels uncomfortable. He retreats underground. Always remember that the rabbit is not the most intelligent animal on earth, but he has been blessed with a very strong sense of instinctive reasoning. These instincts have allowed him to survive for a long time when everything on earth is out to eat him.

More subtle changes in the weather can also cause the cottontail to become subterranean. Cottontails do not like to be pushed when it is very warm or extremely cold. A 75° or 80°F fall day will find most cottontails scurrying for holes once kicked up. The reason is obvious when you're wearing a winter fur coat. Related to this is that fact that fewer rabbits will be kicked up in warm weather because flies and other insects and pests drive them underground.

It is also difficult to jump many rabbits in very cold, 0°F weather, and an awful lot of these are likely to hole quickly. The reason is much the same as if a storm were moving in. The rabbit does not trust the weather or the conditions and wants to stick close to home.

Weather, beyond any other reason, is what forces the bunny to ground. In extreme cases I've seen every run end at the entrance of a ground hog hole. These hunts net few rabbits, and the dogs are loaded up and returned to their pens quickly.

Bad or drastic changes in the weather are the single most important reason why a rabbit holes when being chased. Here Brain Salley shows a nice New York cottontail to Ralphie as a snowstorm moves in.

The Wounded Rabbit. I can't remember a single rabbit that was wounded by the hunter or the dogs that did not attempt to get to some kind of hole. This is surely one time when a rabbit, after passing all kinds of holes, quickly slips into one. And they always seem to know where every hole is! When the rabbit is wounded, his survival instinct takes over again. He knows he is in big trouble and with dogs and the hunter closing in on him, he'll enter any hole, regardless of whether there is another animal in there or not. The rabbit only goes down the hole a short distance in this situation, however. In fact, it is often possible to reach in with a gloved hand and pull him out. This saves the rabbit from being wasted or eaten by the predator.

On a recent hunt, we jumped a big cottontail and he gave the dogs a good chase for ten or fifteen minutes through some fairly open woods. All of a sudden one of my friends cut loose with his double, and yelled, "He's coming down your way, Dave!" Well, the rabbit never showed up, so I walked up and told Jason to walk in where he had shot and look around. As he did this, I saw the rabbit sneak out toward a long fallen tree. Jason fired again and the rabbit disappeared into a hole at the stump end of the tree. Jason believed he hadn't hit the rabbit, but I knew better. There was no reason for him to squeeze into the hole, except for the fact that he was injured in some way.

On a hunt just two days earlier, I rolled two cottontails only to have both escape to holes barely 50 yards away. In each case the dogs and I would have recovered the cottontail if we had had just a few more seconds, but each rabbit knew his territory extremely well and knew the location of every tunnel.

It is rare for me to wound a cottontail, and it may happen only a few times in an entire season. Unfortunately, in the case above, it happened twice in one day. It hammered home the fact that a wounded rabbit, without exception, is going to a hole. If I hit one, or if I only think I hit him, I take up the trail myself and try to stay as close as possible, meanwhile trying to get the dogs there to help me. I have recovered a lot of rabbits this way. If he's wounded, the cottontail is headed for the closest available burrow, and you can bet your new shotgun on it.

No Choice. In some cases the rabbit seems to feel he has no choice but to escape whatever is pursuing him by going underground. In most cases this happens in small woodlots or places where the rabbit has few options. I have noticed that this behavior takes place much more frequently when the rabbit is jumped by the hunter and not the dogs, or the hunter or hunters are talking and making noise. This may sound strange, but rabbits seem to instinctively know that humans are to be feared much more than hounds. If the rabbit does not know the hunter is in the area, he will sometimes institute his normal escape maneuvers and circle the woodlot. But if he knows humans are close by, and dogs are pursuing him, he will often hole up. Sometimes, when I enter a likely looking patch of cottontail habitat, I keep quiet and let the dogs do the work. If the cottontail doesn't know a person is there, the hunter has the advantage and the bunny is less likely to hole up.

Too Much Pressure. Actually this is just another variation of the 'no choice' scenario, but occurs mostly when too many dogs are run in a small area. Dogs are competitive, we all know that. Each wants to be the first to pick up the scent at a check, be the first in line, and so on. This creates a lot of pressure on the rabbit, as dogs become separated, the general pack starts to break down, and hounds flood the woodlot. Too much pressure should not be confused with "dog speed," which is not what we are talking about here. Actually I've also seen rabbits hole up from too much pressure from too many hunters. A rabbit has good ears, he knows when four hunters and a couple of dogs are descending upon him, and he has only an acre or so of good brush in front of him. What would you do? The rabbit quickly decides he had better find a hole, and in most cases he does.

There are many variations on both of these themes of no choice and pressure. Many times the hunter can help the situation by being quiet, running fewer dogs, sometimes hunting with fewer friends, and other things I've mentioned. Of course, it all depends on how serious you want to get about hunting cottontails. Some take the sport more seriously than others, and some are more concerned about just hunting with friends than killing the cottontail, but if you want fewer runs to end with the dogs' noses in a chuckhole, there are a few things you can do about it.

Availability of Holes. There are some areas around my home that I don't even bother hunting anymore. In one place, an overgrown pasture that runs along a railroad bed, cottontail hunting is virtually impossible. There are plenty of cottontails there, but the railroad bed is an easy place for ground hogs to burrow and they have honeycombed the entire bank, as well as the pasture nearby. With so many escape holes, cottontails in the area have learned it is an easy trick to elude any pursuer. You simply cannot hunt there.

Other places are almost as bad. The spot where I mentioned wounding two rabbits in a single day is an old overgrown strip mine. Such old mines also get honeycombed by all kind of burrow makers and sometimes offer incredibly tough hunting. The mines offer good hunting only under ideal weather conditions.

On the other hand, rabbit hunting can be extremely easy in cleared areas and places where the ground is hard and rocky. There are fewer ground hogs and creatures that make holes in the earth in these areas and hence fewer places for rabbits to take refuge. There is a large pine thicket in the mountains where I occasionally run my dogs. Over the years, I have walked every inch of the thicket and can count on one hand the holes I have found there. Consequently the pine thicket offers a great place for run-backs and is easy on the dogs. I don't kill a lot of bunnies there, but I have had some spectacular chases. Swampy areas also provide good hunting because there are very few dry holes there. The availability of holes in the area does have a bearing on the rabbit's decision to use them.

Rabbits go to holes for many reasons. Dog speed and pressure, especially from a single dog, is probably one of the least important reasons why a rabbit suddenly decides to call a halt to the chase. Weather, terrain, and running conditions have a greater influence on a rabbit than the speed of the hound pursuing it.

Dog Speed. There are at least six distinct reasons why rabbits hole up, and I believe dog speed is the least important. I've heard it a million times in the past, and still hear the phrase today, "That dog's too fast. He pushes all the rabbits in the holes!" I don't believe it. I used to, but not anymore.

For the first 16 years or so that I hunted cottontails, I held a full-time job. Free time for hunting was at a premium. I was also a little younger and always in a hurry. I had little use for slow dogs and their "bark every footprint" mentality. I wanted to kill cottontails, and in a hurry, so I got the fastest dogs I could find. Things have slowed down some, but I still like those speedy dogs. What hasn't changed is the fact that just as many rabbits go in holes today as they did then. I've hunted with slow dogs, fast dogs, and everything in between. It doesn't seem to matter to the rabbit what he is being chased by, but it does to the hunter waiting at the other end. If Mr. Cottontail decides he's going to go in the ground today, he goes; if he wants to run all day, then that's what he does; but dog speed alone has little to do with it. I'll admit that occasionally some hounds will pressure a bunny hard enough to force an underground retreat, but usually weather or some other factor helps the bunny decide to go down a woodchuck hole.

I have often said that no dog could ever be too fast for me, and I still hold that belief to some extent. I never worry about the dog's speed pushing rabbits underground; in fact, the only negative thing about a fast dog is that he over-runs the checks and loses the trail. So if you have any dogs that are just too fast, give me a call I can probably use them!

When I began hunting rabbits, it wasn't for any particular reason other than the thrill of the chase and the killing of cottontails. I make no apologies for the fact that I enjoy the entire aspect of it, including the killing. When I'm training a dog or just out exercising him, I have no desire to end the rabbit's life, but when I'm cottontail hunting I want to kill the cottontail, it's just that simple. If it weren't, I'd take up golf or field trialing. In all forms of hunting, the most successful hunters are those who know the most about the quarry they are chasing. Learning why a rabbit circles, or why he holes up, will help you become a better cottontail hunter. It's as simple as that.

13

THE KENNEL

It is a shame that most of us don't get to use our beagles year round, but there are weeks, and sometimes months, when jobs, family responsibilities, and weather keep our hounds confined to their individual pens and cages. No one likes to see his dogs penned up, but in today's world it is a necessity, or the owner would not have his dog very long. Along with thievery, probably the biggest concern facing the dog owner is the real possibility of his important and valuable dog getting hit by a vehicle. It has happened to many of us and it is a tough, heart-wrenching experience. With all this in mind, some reasonable way must be found to keep the dog safe and sound when he is simply resting or experiencing time off from hunting or trials.

There are no limits when building or selecting a kennel for your dogs. I have seen dogs kept on a simple strand of chain, with a steel barrel for cover, and have also seen elaborate concrete kennels complete with septic systems and heated beds. I favor something in between. I'm not very impressed when I see a good gundog using a hot steel barrel for a doghouse, or see a beautiful hound standing in a foot of oozy mud. Then again, spending an excessive amount of money and pampering a dog that is supposed to be a tough hunting hound is not my style either. As I said, I'm sort of in between.

I've tried just about all the known methods of keeping dogs, from chains to fenced concrete runs. I'm not sure there is a perfect system, but the one that works best for me is the off-the-ground kennel that I sometimes call the canine high-rise. The off-the-ground works best with dogs in the beagle size range and has several advantages going for it:

• **It is relatively inexpensive to build.** Depending on how extravagant you get, a good off-the-ground kennel capable of holding two or three dogs can be erected for $300 or less.

• **Security.** Nothing can be more nerve-racking than searching the neighborhood for your expensive beagle or having the neighbors call in the middle of the night to say your dog's loose again. A kennel such as the off-the-ground variety can be locked securely, and even burglar proofed if you feel it necessary.

• **Females in heat seem to attract fewer stray dogs when kept above the ground.** I'm not sure why this is true, as one would think it would just be the opposite, but it has become very clear that this phenomenon does exist. In fact, it is unusual to even see a stray dog around my pens, whether I have a dog in heat or not, and I'm sure it has something to do with them being off the ground.

• **Toughens feet.** If the floor in your kennel is wire or something similar, it will help keep the dogs' feet tough and ready for hunting season.

• **Cleanliness.** I put a lot of time and effort into my dogs and I'm proud of them. When someone stops in, or someone shows up that is interested in buying a dog, I want them to look and smell as nice as possible. The off-the-ground kennel helps do this.

• **Health.** Having a direct relationship to cleanliness--keeping dogs clean, dry, and away from the ground--also keeps the dogs much healthier. Fleas and ticks are kept in check, almost to the point of nonexistence. General health remains good and small problems don't turn into larger ones.

• **Easy clean-up and time saver for the owner.** With all the items combined, the off-the-ground pen simply saves a lot of time that can be used for training or hunting. Pens can be hosed down occasionally, and manure easily hauled away as needed. Other than that, little maintenance is required.

The off-the-ground kennel is not the perfect system for housing dogs, but it does have its advantages. The author has used pens like this one for years with a great deal of success.

Building an Off-the-Ground Kennel

Since new beaglers and persons just getting into the sport will want to know how they can build their own kennel, I will go into detail on how to build an off-the-ground pen. Keep in mind these are just guidelines, and the general concept as well as dimensions can be changed or expanded to suit each individual. The basic structure remains the same, and can be built by anyone with fundamental carpentry skills.

Let's assume you have no building to attach your pen to, and you are basically starting from scratch. Select a location in your yard that will be convenient for you, keeping in mind that there is a strong possibility that you will like this sport of beagling and the off-the-ground pen, and will want to expand. If possible, try to select a spot where the pen will be shaded during the afternoon, or plant fast-growing trees in appropriate locations. I strongly suggest you run a water line and electricity to your kennel or at least have the possibility of adding it later. Lights and water will be a tremendous help for you in caring for the hounds in winter, when the days are very short, as well as during hot, steamy days of summer.

An off-the-ground dog pen under construction. Try to locate the kennel where it will receive some protection form the hot afternoon sun. Notice the water hydrant in left corner, another very good idea.

The basic size of the canine high-rise is roughly ten feet long and slightly less than four feet or 45 inches wide. This is to ensure that wire fencing, which is normally four feet wide, and lengths of eight-foot lumber work into the plan. The pen is suspended from pillars of concrete blocks or six posts of rot-resistant wood. I frequently use short lengths of old utility poles that I pick up along rural roads, as the utility companies are happy to have someone haul them away. I keep the pen suspended relatively high, about two and a half to three feet, so I can easily run the lawn mower under and shovel up the manure.

Once the posts (I normally use six) are set to accept the 10x4-foot pen, I use treated 2x6s, stood on edge for the floor outline. Three feet of one end of the pen facing the weather side will be saved for a deck where the house will be placed. Take into consideration which way wind and rains normally hit your chosen location and build the pen so that the door of the doghouse will face away from this weather side. Keep the deck on this end. You can also enclose and gate the doghouse inside to deter dog-nappers.

Floor supports where the dogs walk are made from one-inch diameter iron or galvanized pipe. Wood simply cannot stand up to the punishment of constantly being doused with water and urine. The lengths of pipe are kept about ten to twelve inches apart, and are notched flush into the main 2x6 with a handsaw. The pipe is cut just a fraction smaller than the outside width dimension.

An additional 2x4 is nailed flush along the outside of the main 2x6 to hold the pipe in place; the floor wire can also be nailed to it. The floor wire is wired directly to the pipe with small pieces of copper wire, and nailed to the wood crosspieces at the end, and at the three-foot line where the deck will begin.

Floor wire should be heavy, one-inch by two-inch welded block. This size allows feces to fall through, and the dogs will walk on it once they get used to it. It is also a good idea and is humane to your dog to add a few running boards for him to walk on. I use two or three one- by four-inch boards down the center of the wire run. I space them a couple inches apart, again so feces will fall through, and wire them directly to the pipe cross members in a few spots. The dogs will use them immediately, and I'm sure would thank you for them if they could. Some kennel builders eliminate the wire in the floor altogether and use treated lumber spaced about an inch apart, saying it is more humane on the dogs.

I have also used expanded metal grating in the two-inch diamond pattern for the floor. This is coated heavily with primer paint and then a couple coats of Rust-oleum paint to cover any sharp edges, and to help preserve it. This floor has worked well for female dogs, but male urine will eat it up in just a few years. Also, some companies are now making plastic kennel floor panels that snap together; these are available at some farm and feed stores. These panels are two by four feet and work well into the kennel plan I am describing. I have used the plastic panels, but the holes are very tight. Some states, including Pennsylvania, are now requiring kennel operators to use the plastic floor, although I have had no problems with dogs on the metal floors.

Any size wire can be used on the sides and top. Yes, do yourself a favor and wire the top or put on a good solid roof. An ambitious dog will chew through anything to get out. After early problems, I make it a practice to wire the roof and then put any roof material on top of the wire. Some dogs will simply destroy anything that is not covered, but they can't chew through welded wire!

Uprights for the sides should be between 32 and

One-inch diameter pipe can be used for floor supports. Wood will not stand up as well in the floor. It is a matter of personal preference, however, and some kennel owners do use wood, metal grating, and even newer plastic panels.

36 inches high. All the lumber should be treated and then given a couple additional coats of oil-based paint. The idea is for the pen to be relatively maintenance free and last for at least ten years.

After years of seeing my dogs lying around on top of their houses, I hit upon the idea of adding a perch or shelf at the end of the wire run for the dogs to lounge around on. The dogs absolutely love it. The sturdy perch also adds more usable space for the dogs, and creates a place for one dog to get away from an aggressive one or a pesky pup. Some dogs soon create a game out of chasing each other up and down from these benches, which gives them much needed exercise.

To make a perch in your kennel, simply run a couple 2x4s across the uprights at end of the wire run about 15 inches from the floor. Span across the pen with a few furring strips onto the 2x4s and cover with a piece of half-inch plywood. If you have some one-inch sheeting or rough lumber you can tack them tight together and eliminate the plywood. A nice size perch that holds two dogs is 20 to 24 inches wide, while the entire width of the kennel is about 45 inches. Your dogs will love this little addition to their home, and you won't be sorry you took the time to build it.

A good place for a door or gate in the off-the-ground kennel is right in the middle of the wire run. This will enable you to reach almost the entire inner area, to catch a stubborn dog, or retrieve a pan that gets shoved into a corner. I usually throw in a 2x4 header over the door, and a doorsill made out of a scrap of 2x8. This helps keep the door smaller and gives something solid for the dogs to stand on when you open the pen to pet them or administer medication. I keep my gates about 25 inches high by 20 inches wide. This size seems to fit all the needs that come up, and I can even squeeze in if the need arises to make a repair or catch an unruly dog.

Gates are made out of any leftover lumber. I normally rip a few 2x4 pieces in half and use the 2x2 pieces for the top, bottom, and maybe a center brace. This makes nailing together easier, and keeps the gate as light as possible. You can also use a few window gussets at the corners for added strength. The gate is then wired with whatever is left over, but I like to use the smaller floor wire (1x2 inches) as it is easier to work with and does a nice neat job. The wire also helps make the gate very sturdy. The new door is also fitted with a pair of four- or five-inch hinges, and a good, heavy barrel-bolt lock.

The completed off-the-ground kennel offers the dogs a clean, comfortable, and secure place to live when they are not hunting. It may not be perfect but it fulfills all the dog's requirements better than a chain and metal barrel.

If you've never done it before, making the gate can take as long as building the rest of the pen! The secret is to plan ahead. Know precisely where you want the gate, put in two uprights at this location, and keep them nice and straight. Keep the gate square, and make it a good inch or so (even more up and down) smaller than the opening. Use a good solid piece of one by four tacked along the inside of the lock upright for a doorstop to keep the gate from swinging in. It is not difficult, and anyone can do it with a little planning.

Once the general pen is complete and wired, all that needs to be finished is the deck that will accept the doghouse. After trying several pens with built-in houses, I found it was easier to keep the house totally separate. This allows you to replace houses quickly, switch them around to suit different dogs, clean them out easily, and also makes the general appearance of the kennel better. Of course the builder can, once again, build whatever he thinks will suit him (and his dog). I have tried a lot of pens and styles before I came up with one that eliminated most of my problems. If you want to place the doghouse inside and eliminate the deck you can, but you have to "gate" that end so it will fit. I have built both types.

If you decide to build the deck, the platform is made out of about eight treated 2x4s, spaced one inch apart. I simply place a scrap piece of 2x4 block between each one for spacing, knock the next one to it, and tack it down. I also do the same along the edge, letting the deck hang over an inch to match the rest of the pen. An appropriate doghouse is slid into place on the center of the deck, and the end wire is cut out where the house opening is. It gets pretty cold here in Pennsylvania, and we usually see a few days of below-zero weather each winter. With the deck three feet by almost four feet, there is room enough to stack a few bales of hay around the house, and you can set the house right on some type of insulation for added warm. Before I built my barn kennel, I used to keep extra feeding pans, insect spray, medication, collars, leashes, and other gear in watertight containers right on the decks.

Since this book is not about building kennels and doghouses, it wouldn't be prudent to go into detail about building doghouses. A wooden structure with a shingled roof fits the bill better than anything else and the average person can build one without much difficulty. Most lumberyards and hardware stores will supply you with plans for doghouses. Also, since dogs are popular pets and pastimes, many small businesses that build garages and other buildings have begun to make doghouses too. A good wooden house, as mentioned, sells for around $50 and up. Many times, it is more economical to buy one than to track down and buy all the materials, and build it yourself. There are also many new, durable plastic houses on the market now, and I have used both; wood and plastic.

If you've followed some of my directions you should now have a good secure kennel to house your favorite hound. One drawback to the off-the-ground kennel that I have observed over the years is that the dogs' toenails tend to grow rapidly, and they don't wear them off while walking on the wire. This is really no big deal, as nails can be clipped periodically in just a few minutes.

Another definite drawback to the off-the-ground kennel is obvious; the dog simply does not have much room to move around and exercise. This doesn't seem to be a problem with two young pups, as they will tear in and out of the house, chase each other up and down the perch, and tire each other out. I've taken advantage of this excess puppy energy by placing a frisky pup in with dogs that have a tendency to get lazy. The pup simply harasses the older dog, and he is constantly on the move to get away from the little pest. With older dogs, however, the need for the dog to get out as much as possible, even during the non-hunting season, is a real concern.

With an off-the-ground kennel, the dog is also literally suspended in air, and one might wonder if it has any effect on the dog's balance or his "feel" for the ground once he is placed back on earth. I've never had any problems with this, and the dogs adapt to the wire amazingly well. Again, we should keep in mind that all dogs should get some exercise out of the kennel whenever possible. I will be the first to admit my dogs need out more during the offseason, but sometimes work or days of severe weather just won't allow it. I try to let mine down as much as I can, even if it is just for a few minutes at feeding time.

The off-the-ground kennel has worked well for me over the years, but it is not perfect housing for our dogs. Only our imagination and our available funds limit improvements in any kennel system. Don't be afraid to experiment if you think you have a better idea. I've always felt that we owe it to the dogs to build the best possible home we can for them.

Improvements in any kennel are limited only by your imagination. The author constructed this off-the-ground one using expanded metal for the floor and roofing the entire three-section pen including the dog houses. Bowser says he likes it!

Other Variations in Housing

There are other good, sound methods for keeping your dogs, and they should not be overlooked. As the years have gone by, I have built a kennel barn and attached some runs to this barn and cut holes in the side of the building for the dogs to enter and exit. Each dog has his own box inside the barn and also has access to the partitioned run outside. Many kennels are built this way, and it is a good, sound way to house dogs. I can keep all my gear, collars, feed, and so on inside, dry and out of the weather, and still have access to some of the dogs. I can even feed some of the dogs inside out of the weather.

A variation that is becoming more and more popular is simply setting up a barn-type storage shed and fastening off-the-ground runs, or fenced ground runs to it. The storage shed can be partitioned off for individual dogs, and the remaining area is used for feed, tools, and accessories. The entire shed becomes the kennel, and I fashioned my barn kennel from this basic idea. It is this type of setup, where doghouses are essentially eliminated and the entire building can be heated in cold weather, that appeals to me.

Pennsylvania winters can be brutal so as the author's interest in rabbit hunting and beagling increased, he finally built a barn-type kennel in 1995. It allows the storage of feed, etc. inside out of the weather, and allows inside access to some of the dogs (see next picture).

One variation in housing for your hound is to fasten an off-the-ground pen directly to a building. This allows the dogs to come inside, eliminates dog houses, and keeps everything safe and dry. Kennel design is limited only by your imagination.

Another variation along this same theme is the concrete block kennel with concrete runs attached to it. This type of kennel offers the ultimate in dog luxury, and convenience for the operator. Again, each dog has his own run or exercise area, runs being made of poured concrete, and his own inside bedding area. Each exercise run is usually slopped to a central drain, and urine and waste is carried to a cleanable tank or an underground septic system. This type of kennel is usually owned by a professional dog breeder, and in many cases is well suited to the larger breeds of dogs. It should be no surprise that this type of kennel is expensive to build, and the sky is the limit on what you could spend. I certainly see nothing wrong with having one if the dog owner has the resources and is serious about his dogs. In most cases when someone begins to contemplate a structure-type kennel, his interest in the hounds has become more than just a hobby.

I gave it much thought before building a kennel similar to the one described. I never have more than a dozen dogs at a time, and have been able to accommodate them well in several off-the-ground pens over the years. Since my interest in cottontail hunting and beagling has continued to grow in recent years, however, I found more of a need for a permanent block kennel. Pennsylvania winters can be brutal, and long periods of frozen water pans and hoses kept getting more frustrating the older I got. The fact that these building-type kennels can be heated in severe weather was very appealing, especially now that I am keeping more hounds. However, the average beagle owner who has one or two dogs will rarely see the need or sense for a multi-thousand dollar kennel. The point is to build what you feel you need, and spend what you can afford.

In my video, *Cottontail Rabbit Hunting*, I mention the fact that our dogs become more than tools to kill rabbits with. They become friends, companions, and in some cases members of the family. I think the minute we become dog owners we almost become parents. We accept the responsibility to care for and meet all the dog's needs. It should be obvious that the domesticated hound can no longer care for himself. I believe we owe it to the dog to give him the most comfortable living quarters we possibility can; a steel barrel and six-foot piece of chain just doesn't make it. "Once in a while put yourself in the dog's place . . ."

When we become dog owners we almost become parents. We owe it to the dog to give him the most comfortable living quarters we possibility can. Here Buster thanks Dave for taking care of him!

The intensity of the scent on a trail is determined by the amount of body odor the rabbit leaves either in prints, suspended in the air, or on bushes and things he makes contact with.

14

MAKING SENSE OUT OF SCENTS

id you ever wonder how the dogs could come across a fresh rabbit track and tear off at full speed in the right direction? Sure you have, and if you've hunted rabbits for more than a couple days, you've no doubt marveled at this peculiar beagle trait. It's obvious we can't ask the dogs, and the most popular solution to this mystery is simply the scent is stronger in the direction the rabbit is going. Well, that makes sense, but since we can't ask the dogs, I think this particular talent will always be somewhat of a mystery.

Tons of material have been written in these pages about the beagles' conformation, his breeding, running speed, etc., but without a fairly good nose, the beagles' worth as a hunting hound is pretty much zero. There are a few that seem to sneak by while trailing behind some other dog, but most of the time, a beagle without the minimal nasal gear is quickly destroyed.

I read somewhere that a dog's nose can process information (in the form of smells and scents) about a million times better than we humans can. Again, we can't ask the dogs, but if you've ever watched a good dog trail a rabbit over solid, frozen ground or across a hard-topped road, you would have to admit they have some smeller on them!

There are a hundred factors that determine good, or bad scenting conditions, and I won't even begin to try to cover them all here. Experienced beaglers know that terrain, temperature, barometric pressure, type of cover; time of day, wind conditions, and all kinds of other things can effect how well our dogs can run a rabbit. In fact, I write this on a day when I know the rabbits are holed up and scent conditions are so tough, it is simply easier to rest the dogs, wait for a change. It is 11 degrees below zero, and the wind is whipping about 15 miles per hour! Not ideal hunting conditions for me or a beagle!

After many years of hunting, I am still unsure of the ideal scenting conditions. Sometimes when you think conditions are right, no dog is "locked on" like you hoped they would be. If I have my choice, I like to hunt after several days of cold, frosty weather, and with a spotty, melting snowpack. This does two things. First, it assures some rabbits will be sitting out after a few days underground. Second, with the damp ground and melting snow, I know scent will be clinging pretty well to the ground, and the snow will be stuck down enough so the dogs will not suck in up their nostrils. If the snowpack is melting and spotty, as I've described, it's going to allow the dogs to speed up and keep pressure on the rabbit when they hit open ground. To kill rabbits, the dog (any dog) has to keep pressure on the rabbit. A "dawdler" gives that rabbit time to twist, turn, and make the chase far more complicated than it should be. Throw in a nice, overcast day with the temperature about 38 degrees, and you have the ingredients for a perfect rabbit hunt.

I can't speak for those in the south, but our worse scenting days are those when the ground is frozen hard, or we have several inches of icy, grainy-type snow. On these days, the dogs just can't seem to lock onto any scent and we usually have poor hunting days. Some types of snow have much less effect on dogs, and I have noticed my dogs ran rather well during the late 1998-1999 season on three or four inches of soft, almost powdery snow. With mild winters becoming more and more common, this particular winter had snow on for much of the season. I should add here, however, that experience also has much to do with this. As a dog gets older and has been on a lot of hunts, he is more able to unravel the tiny bit of scent he may be getting up his nose. Older dogs with a few brains also learn to simply follow the tracks in the snow, picking up what scent he can, but also sighting the next set of tracks ahead of him. It may not be textbook, but it gets the job done. Generally, snow that will roll up (as in building a snowman!), makes pretty good hunting.

It's pretty clear that scent freezes. Consider deer, or fish frozen solid in the freezer; you don't smell anything when you sniff at the packages, but lay those packages out on the counter and by the end of the day the whole house smells. It's the same with scent or smell given off by game and in this case rabbits.

The bunny hops around during the early morning hours before dawn and as he goes along it takes only a few minutes to freeze his footprints locking in his scent. The hound comes along a few hours later and as the sun begins to warm the ground the tracks begin to thaw releasing the scent. Sometimes when you are out hunting you can literally see the steam slowly coming up from frozen ground. This is the exact principle and the bunny scent is drifting up from the prints, and although we can't see it, the dog can smell it clearly. He may begin to cold–trail because he has no way of knowing the scent was laid down hours before.

Temperature does have a lot to do with scenting conditions and how the ground reacts to them. My friend Al, from Pine Bush, New York, is a life-long rabbit hunter and likes to get up at the crack of dawn. When I hunted with him, we were in the woods long before the morning thaw and conditions weren't very good for running. Since his winters are much more severe than ours in Pennsylvania, I suggested Al delay the hunt a little. Al has now told me, "We've been going out later in the morning, and doing very well in the afternoon . . . it's easier on the dogs, and it's been keeping us hunting. We'll sleep in a little later next time you come!"

A temperature above freezing, along with a lower barometric pressure is definitely going to make for better scenting conditions. There is a limit to this, however, and it should be no mystery that once the ground gets hard, dry, and baked, scenting is going to go the other way. Here in the north, it's easy to see smoke from wood burners "hanging" in the air and floating into valleys. These are better scenting days. Tough, clear, cold weather conditions make this same smoke go straight up and dissipate quickly. Rabbit scent will do the same thing.

Wind, terrain and lots of other factors also determine how well our beagles can run a rabbit. When I hunted with Zef Selca, in up state New York, I was amazed to watch his dogs running "downwind" of the actual track. I had never seen this in a rabbit dog, and it took me a few minutes to figure it out. At first, I thought these dogs can't even stay on the track, but quickly learned that to run the hare at the speed they did, it was the only way they could run him! The dogs simply galloped along in the ten inches of snow grabbing the scent about eight to ten feet downwind. It was something to see. I am sure this is nothing new to guys that run hares a lot.

Two years ago, we had so much snow we rarely ran on bare ground after Thanksgiving. My dogs did better than expected, and late in the season I also saw them running slightly downwind of the actual track. My hounds have always been only fair at best in the snow, but I think it was that "experience" factor again. They were run so much on snow; they adapted and struggled to find someway of keeping the chase going. It worked and we had one of our best seasons ever despite pitiful weather sometimes.

Good dogs will always find some way to adapt to the conditions and terrain. Most of us have seen a pack tearing it up through nice soft weeds, slow down in tough multi-flora rose, and go very slow over hard packed ground or up a dirt road. Sometimes all of these conditions can be found on a single run!

Here in western Pennsylvania where I live, we have some really varied conditions. Some of our hunts take place in and around old strip mines where the dogs may be called upon to start the rabbit in a corn field, press him across a

A dog can process smells and scents about a million times better than his human counterpart. Did you ever wonder how a dog can come across a fresh rabbit track and tear off in the right direction?

few acres of heavy briars, then scale a 30 foot vertical wall, and trail over loose shale rock. It's a crazy chase sometimes, and we hole and lose a lot of rabbits, but sometimes you have to be impressed when the dogs stick to it over all these varied scenting conditions until the rabbit is killed.

On some of these chases, it is not hard to see when the dogs are going well, and when they are having a tough time. Dogs seem to run a few different types of scent that the rabbit lays down. Most of the time the dogs are trailing "footprints" and other times they are running "body scent."

When my dogs are having a tough time running across open ground and I can see they are heading back to thicker brush, I know the chase is going to heat up once they get back to the cover. The rabbit simply leaves more scent as he brushes up against stuff, besides leaving good footprint scent. The dogs are able to get more scent, work less, and simply go faster.

Dogs will run body scent, footprint scent, or air scent or a combination of all depending on the air and ground conditions. The dog has one thing in mine . . . follow the rabbit, and in almost all cases he'll use his nose to somehow get the job done. I have a couple good "jump dogs" in my pack, and they are useful, but it is the ones with the good noses that make for some spectacular rabbit chases. We all know that a dog that can dig around and produce a rabbit, and is equipped with a good enough nose to push that rascal around is a valuable dog to anyone.

Rabbits also put down a lot of scent, or little at all depending again on weather, and other conditions. I am sure most of us have seen how difficult it is for our dogs to run a young or very small rabbit. On the other hand with some large, buck rabbits it seems like the dogs can never lose them. Again, it's the amount of body odor the rabbit leaves either in prints, suspended in the air or, on bushes and things he makes contact with.

We have run hare in Michigan when the scent was so strong, I swear I could have run that rabbit! We make jokes about it sometimes, but if the conditions are right, and you come across a big smelly hare . . . a poodle could probably bring the thing around to the gun. The wrench in the whole scheme of things is when snow comes and changes everything. So, I would leave the poodle at home!

Before I wrap up this chapter, I would like to reiterate that weather and how it affects the ground conditions is certainly the greatest factor in how much scent the dog can recover and process, transferring this information into his own running style to keep the rabbit moving. I have what I feel are some very good dogs and we kill a lot of rabbits in front of them. But there are days when I would sell the whole bunch for $10! So don't blame the dog, sometimes he's doing the best he can, even though it might not satisfy us.

A good hunting hound should have one goal in mind, to press the quarry hard enough to overtake him. This means see the rabbit, fox, coyote, whatever, killed by the hunter or caught by him or his pack mates. You can disagree if you like, but that's what they were bred for, and a good dog still has this ancient instinct instilled in him. If he doesn't he will never be a great tracking hound.

To do all this that we ask of him, he has to have a good, working nose on him. Can you imagine the scents of pine needles, leaves, old 'possum tracks, swamp water, deer, weeds, flowers, our own aftershave, and hundreds of other smells he has to siff through to pick up that one distinguishable scent of a rabbit!? In the end, he is the only one that can make any sense out of all those scents!

Some rabbits live in brushy, thorny terrain where a dog may get thorns and briar spines in his feet.

15

CARING
FOR YOUR BEAGLE

S urprisingly, your new hunting hound will require very little attention and is by nature a hardy and healthy breed. During the offseason when he is not hunting, few problems will pop up, but as soon as he is called on to run rabbits day after day in all kinds of terrain and weather, the chances of him injuring himself or getting sick and run down go up drastically.

Experience is always the best teacher, and once the new beagler encounters a problem, providing it is not too serious, he will learn from it and have some idea how to deal with it the next time. My best advice is don't be afraid to tend to the dog's general needs. Learn to cut his toenails, administer medications, and perform treatments that you know are in his best interest. **USE COMMON SENSE**. If you return from a hunt with your dog soaking wet and noticeably cold and chilling, don't be afraid to bring him inside, towel him dry, and give him something warm to eat. This is not pampering the dog; this is using common sense. Remember, there is a good chance the dog will be called upon to hunt the next day, and he will be of little use for days if he develops a cold and fever.

This is the general care we are talking about, heading off minor problems before they cause major headaches; care that the dog owner should be knowledgeable in, and ready to deal with. I don't think it is necessary to take your dog to a vet for every tiny problem or ailment, but the dog owner shouldn't experiment, either. When you encounter a problem you are sure is beyond the scope of your abilities, don't hesitate; get the dog to a vet, quickly. Also, have a veterinarian in mind or chosen ahead of time. Know his specialties, his office hours, and his home phone if available. It could mean life or death to your dog.

Parasitic Worms

Let's assume that you will not perform brain surgery on your new hunting dog, but will do everything possible to keep him healthy and chasing rabbits. General care begins the minute you bring the new puppy home. Always assume that any new puppy is carrying some type of worms, and worm him as a preventive measure. Left untreated, parasitic worms will sap the life from your pup and in many cases kill him.

Worms are easily detected by a dull, dirty-looking coat; a bloated stomach most of the time, not just after eating; extremely foul-smelling and runny stool; and sometimes the actual worms visible in stool or rectum. Worms are in most cases easy to get rid of, but left to grow and multiply they can cause total bile block in puppies and full-grown dogs. Excellent worm capsules are available at pet, feed, and department stores or from mail-order suppliers of dog products. Powders and liquids that can be added directly to food are also available and easy to use. In extreme cases, your vet can dispense even more powerful drugs or give injections directly into the bile. Again, worms are not a serious problem unless left untreated. Assume every puppy is a carrier, and worm/treat him.

Since worm infestations know no age limits, puppies and other dogs can transmit worms to older, otherwise healthy dogs. Working, hunting dogs can also pick up worms in the field. I routinely worm my dogs (and notice worms) immediately at the end of each split hunting season, and once or twice throughout the rest of the year.

The most common parasitic worms that the dog owner will be dealing with are stomach worms, commonly called roundworms; tapeworms; hookworms; whipworms; and heartworms. In all cases, prevention is worth all the effort spent on a cure once the dog is infected. Keep kennels clean, feed good nutritional food, develop a regular worming program, and don't expose your hound unduly to stray and infected dogs, and you will save yourself a major headache in dealing with most of these pests. In the process you will have a healthy, energetic dog that wants to hunt instead of a mopping, lazy hound that only acts this way because his strength is being drained from him by some hidden parasite.

We are fortunate today, as science and major drug companies have made dealing with dog worms extremely easy, contrary to years ago when, in some cases, there was no known cure, or the knowledge to know what was even causing the affliction. An explanation of the life and habits of each individual type of worm would serve no purpose and is of little interest to the beagle owner. Once he surmises his dog is infected, he will care little about the name or type of worm, but how to get rid of it. That is not to say that sometimes the identification of a worm will aid in its removal, as it surely will, and therefore we will briefly describe each parasite commonly found in hunting dogs.

Roundworms are "round" in appearance, a few inches long, and white, smooth, and shiny. Dog owners commonly call these spaghetti worms. They are easily seen in stool or vomit, or the vet will encounter their eggs under the microscope. There are many products on the market designed to combat round-worms, and they are one of the easiest infestations to get rid of.

Hookworms are much smaller, barely half an inch long, and difficult to detect by the kennel owner, but they are picked up by the vet when examining stool. Hookworms get their name from the small tentacles or "hooks" they use to cling to the intestine wall. They can suck a tremendous amount of blood from the dog host, causing rapid weight loss. A general decline in the dog's health, and sometimes death, may indicate the presence of hookworms when no other sign of demise will be noticed.

Whipworms resemble a whip, with a short stubby base and long thin lash. They generally attach themselves to the large intestine and require several treatments of medicine before they are eliminated. An enema with a veterinarian-prescribed drug may be needed. Drugs such as diethylcarbamazine and oxibendazole also keep whipworms in check.

Any rabbit hunter who has examined the entrails of just a few rabbits can

Tapeworm eggs can be easily ingested by a hound just licking the kill. Make an effort to keep your dogs away from rabbit entrails.

readily describe the common tapeworm. It is a long, yellowish, segmented worm that wraps itself around the intestine. It is said that each segment is capable of growing a new and complete worm. It sucks the blood and the energy from many victims. At the anal opening of almost every cottontail will be found the rice-like globs of clear jelly containing the eggs or dormant stage of the tapeworm. When ingested by an innocent hound just licking the kill, they will grow inside the dog into an adult worm. Modern medications will kill the tapeworm, but sometimes it takes several treatments and a trip to the vet. The accepted drug for tapeworm is arecoline bromide. The best defense, especially where beagles are concerned, is keeping your hound away from the rabbits' entrails.

Over the past decade or so, heartworms, another worm parasite, have cropped up to become a problem to dog owners in many parts of the country. I am skeptical about its severity, and sometimes feel that drug companies and veterinarian supply houses sell vaccines, medications, and treatments that actually exaggerate problems.

Heartworms are a mysterious ailment, because the life cycle of the parasite is complicated and the dog can be infected for years before symptoms develop. The adult heartworm, *Dirofilaria immitis*, develops in the heart. Even experts disagree on how the dog is actually infected. Some say the mosquito carries the larvae stage on its mouth parts. When the mosquito goes to feed again, the larvae are deposited on the dog, where they burrow into tissue and slowly become small adult worms. These small worms enter a vein and migrate to the heart. Others say the mosquito injects the juvenile stage (microfilariae) directly into the bloodstream, and these immature worms imbed themselves in the heart and slowly grow into adults. In either case, the mosquito is definitely involved and is the major carrier. Once in the heart, the worms begin to destroy the valves and pulmonary artery. In time the adults spawn new live young (microfilariae), and they are carried throughout the bloodstream. Along comes a mosquito, bites the dog, and carries the disease to the next victim, and the process starts all over again.

Despite my skepticism in some cases, heartworm is a serious disease and should not be taken lightly. Here in the North, where winters kill most mosquitoes, heartworm is not a common ailment, but we do have cases, even in my own county. As is the case in all the parasitic infections, prevention is the best defense against heartworms. Since it would be virtually impossible to keep our dogs away from mosquitoes, drugs are the only defense. Ivermectin and other drugs will at least prevent heartworms from gaining a foothold, as once infected a dog could suffer irreversible heart damage. Newer drugs can now be administered once a month or longer and have made dealing with heartworms much easier. Blood tests (sometimes it takes several) will discover the heartworm disease. If you live in swampy or coastal areas, or if you suspect heartworms, see your veterinarian. Diagnosis is difficult, but treatment is becoming easier.

Administering Oral Medications

Sooner or later, either to get rid of worms or assist in controlling some other ailment, you're going to have to give your dog medications. Some come in liquid form, powder, tablets, or capsules. Most of the powders and liquids can be mixed in food or drink and the problem is over, but sometimes the medicine is better if given full strength. Other times the dog simply won't eat.

In these cases the liquid or pill must be forced down the beagle's throat. Again, this is no problem with some dogs, as they will only mildly protest. With some other dogs, however, this can be a nightmare. If the medication is liquid and the dog won't take it, siphon the appropriate dose into a syringe containing no needle. With the dog standing or sitting beside you, come down over the top of his muzzle with your hand, slowly slipping your fingers in one side of his mouths and your thumb in the other side. Beagles are generally small enough to open their mouth with one hand. Once your fingers are in the space directly behind the canine teeth, the dog will open his mouth or you'll simply have to pry open his mouth with as much force as is required. It will be difficult for the dog to bite you, and beagles are not very aggressive, but be careful. In tough cases, you may have to use a leather glove, but I've never found it necessary. Once the dog's mouth is open, squirt the medication in the back of his throat with your other hand, remove your fingers, and allow the dog to swallow. With liquid medication he has almost no choice but to swallow it.

Pills can be another story, and some hounds will drive you to the brink of insanity trying to get them to take their medicine. I truly believe some actually make a game out of it, learning not to swallow for what seems like eternity or to craftily hide the pill in their mouth until you walk away. My male dog Buster and I played this game for years, and he was an expert at it.

The procedure is the same. Pry his mouth open with one hand, but this time you must shove the pill far enough down his throat so he can't spit it back out. This is where the fun begins. I generally toss the pill in; then, using the index finger of my right hand (I'm holding the dog's mouth open with my left), I hook this finger into the rear corner of the dog's mouth and shove the pill on down. If everything goes right, I shove the pill down so far and so fast that the hound just can't get it back up. Once the pill is in, quickly clamp his mouth shut, slowly stroke his throat, and wait for him to swallow. Sometimes, this can take a few seconds or, in some instances, even several minutes.

During this whole procedure, keep in mind that this must be done and that you are doing no harm to the dog. Two minutes later the dog will seem to have forgotten the whole episode. Also, the amount of effort required to administer pills will depend on the dog. My dog, Buster, was an exception, and most dogs take pills easily. Another dog, Sue-Sue, was required to take medication every-day of her life. Fortunately she ate the pills out of my hand without any per-suasion.

Vaccinations

When your pup is between six and eight weeks old, he must be vaccinated against the common dog diseases. I say "must" because there is no discussion on this. A hunting dog's real purpose is hunting, which means he won't be confined to a cage or protective sterile environment. He'll inevitably be running where other unvaccinated dogs have been, and also be in direct contact with wild ani-mals and other individuals.

For a long time, I didn't get my hounds vaccinated. I was lucky. One day my vet pointed out that I was playing Russian roulette with my dogs' lives. I had no argument, because he was right. In the weeks ahead I got all my dogs the appro-priate shots. A short time later parvo arrived on the scene, and it killed many dogs in my area, including several at a neighbor's. I did have a couple pups get mildly sick, but since the mother had been vaccinated and the pups were still sucking they survived. None of my other dogs showed any signs of illness. Needless to say, I have practiced a regular vaccinating schedule since then.

Unless there is a specific problem in your area, vaccinations fall into two cat-egories: rabies and "the others." Simplifying this further, a rabies vaccine is usu-ally a singular, separate dose injected into the muscle of the hind leg. The rabies vaccine comes in one-, three-, and five-year doses. There are some variations to this, as there are rabies vaccines that can be given under the skin, but the most accepted method is a three-year shot given intramuscularly (in the muscle).

The second shot is a combination shot and carries the virus of parvo, hepati-tis, distemper, and perhaps as many as four other diseases. The combination shots are administered subcutaneously, or under the skin. With these two injections, the hound is pretty well protected against the diseases that will try to attack him.

Vaccines for kennel cough and other specific diseases are also available, but in most cases the dog or kennel owner will have a specific need for them. Kennel cough, a disease where the dog develops a disgusting raspy cough, is only par-tially preventable, and a good combination shot carries virus designed to immu-nize against it. There is no known cure for the kennel cough, probably because it is thought to be caused by a combination of several viruses interacting together. Fortunately, I have had no encounters with the disease, but I understand that in some parts of the country it is such a problem that owners vaccinate especially for it, giving the dog specific doses of the viruses known to be present in infected dogs of that area. The best way to prevent kennel cough is to keep your dogs away from dogs that are infected. It spreads easily.

There are two ways for your dog to receive his vaccinations: see a vet, or learn to give them yourself. In the beginning, I routinely took my dogs to the vet for their vaccinations. Then I only had three or four dogs, but still ended up with a hefty vet bill. Each dog receives two shots and the vet charges about $10 (or a lot more) a shot. Four dogs equal $80. In addition, I normally had a couple minor problems that needed looked after, and also bought medications there. I rarely left the office without my wallet $100 lighter, and the bill going up every year. Now that I have ten dogs - well, you can do the math. I had to find another way.

The other way was simply buying vaccines and dog-care products from companies that advertised in my hound and outdoor publications. Vaccines come packed in cooled boxes (in a couple days) complete with instructions on how to use them. At the present time, I can vaccinate for less than $5 a shot. The procedure is not difficult, and you can learn it easily. However, if you have only one or two dogs, and you feel the yearly expense is justified, or you may be a little hesitant about sticking needles in your dog, you may want to continue regular vet visits, and I see nothing wrong with this.

The only drawback to self-administered vaccines is that the dog receives no valid health certificate from a vet. In the event the dog must be shipped out of state, he will have to be re-vaccinated (by a vet) to receive a certificate. Also, since a licensed veterinarian has not vaccinated the dog, local officials may not acknowledge his vaccination should the dog bite someone. Legally, the dog owner will be held responsible, with or without a rabies vaccination certificate, so I've never considered this a problem. If you have more than a few dogs and are concerned more about their health than shipping them out of the state, I believe that home vaccinations are the way to go.

Okay, let's assume you've decided to vaccinate your own dogs, have secured a catalogue, made your choices, and now have the appropriate serums in front of you. Read the directions carefully, but to help others decide if this is for them, we'll go through the inoculation procedure. This will bolster confidence, and after the initial time it will seem an easy task.

In many cases, the rabies vaccine arrives in a single-dose syringe plunger. Needles are purchased separately for a few cents extra. Snap a needle onto the syringe and you're almost ready to give your first shot. Hold the syringe upright, tap it gently to get any air bubbles to rise toward the needle shaft, and carefully press the plunger until all the air is forced out and the vaccine begins to squirt out.

Select a site on the dog's rear leg that is big and meaty. Most instructions recommend the space between the hip and knee. You may also want to clean the area around the site with alcohol. Insert the needle into the muscle and pull back on the plunger slightly. This is called "aspirating," and is a check to see if the needle has entered a blood vessel. If blood begins to appear in the syringe when you aspirate, withdraw the needle, and select another site.

I recommend you follow the supplier's directions to the letter. You will need to be comfortable with giving the shots, especially when you are just starting out. There is little to go wrong here.

Once the needle is in and you've decided it is not in a vessel, push the plunger slowly and smoothly, injecting all the serum. Pull the needle out quickly and you've just given your first dog shot. The entire procedure takes but a few seconds. The rabies vaccine burns in the muscle and some dogs may whine and squirm a little, while some pay little attention to what you're doing to them. I always have a helper hold the dog securely, and I massage the leg muscle for a few seconds after the injection.

Collar tags and certificates come with the rabies vials, but here again they will not be valid unless signed by a registered veterinarian. Fill out the certificates anyway and keep them with your other dog papers. You will then have a record of the vaccination and all the information pertaining to it. Collar tags do remind you, and everyone else, that your dog has been protected against rabies.

Combination shots are given subcutaneously, or under the skin. This is easier in beagles than most breeds because of their loose floppy skin. Combination shots usually come in two separate vials and must be mixed. Don't panic, as this is an easy, simple procedure. One vial contains a liquid with some of the virus suspended in it, and the other contains the other viruses in a tiny freeze-dried cube.

One note of caution. Always use a new, sterile needle for each injection. They cost but pennies, and ensure against an abscess or infection around the injection site. With a clean, fresh needle, turn the liquid vial upside down and insert the needle tip through the rubber cap, pull back on the plunger, and withdraw all the liquid into the syringe. Pierce the cap of the second vial with the needle, push the plunger, and inject the liquid. The cube will dissolve instantly. Shake the vial to mix thoroughly, and then withdraw the entire contents back into the syringe. You're ready for shot number two.

Hold the syringe upright as before, expelling any air that may have collected while mixing. Select a site, this time on the back of the neck just behind the collar. Hold up the skin, insert the needle under the skin layer, aspirate and inject. You've just given your second dog shot, and your hound is safe to roam your favorite bunny patch.

Since the viruses you've injected are designed to actually give your dog a mild case of the disease it is intended to protect against, he may get sick for a few days or just may not act like his normal self. In fact, there is a remote chance that his immune system cannot handle one of the diseases and he may die. Veterinarians protect themselves against this unlikely occurrence by requesting dog owners sign a form relinquishing them of responsibility. I guess nothing is without risk, but the advantages of inoculation far outweigh the chances of your dog dying because of a vaccination. In these rare and extreme cases, it is likely the dog had some hidden problem in the first place. His life on earth was probably in serious jeopardy before the shot was given.

Puppies should receive their first inoculations around seven or eight weeks of age. Rabies shots are effective for three years, but most manufacturers suggest a second shot when the pup is a year old. The pup should receive at least three seven-way or combination shots during his first year, and then at least one every year afterwards. I follow this schedule fairly close, making sure my older dogs receive at least one combination shot every year.

Once you have any worm infestations under control and your beagle has been given his appropriate vaccinations, he will require little hands-on medical treatment. There will be some general care items that are tied directly to simple hygiene, and minor injuries from hunting and other activities that you can usually take care of yourself.

Dogs in general are truly amazing animals. They fight, kick, scream, and hate what you're doing to them at the time, but don't think for one minute that they don't realize you're helping them. My dog, Buster, fought me all his life when I tried to give him medication or dig a thorn out of his paw or just give him a bath. He knew it was for his own good and once in awhile he'd give in, but he'd still protest. But when he wanted or needed something, he would come looking for me holding up a hurt paw or panting for a cool drink. He knew who took care of him. His son, Ralphie, was the same way, and when he was seriously injured in The Laurel Swamp, he came to me instantly for help.

Bathing Your Dog

Nothing will head off problems better than keeping your hound, his eating pans and living space as clean as possible. Don't be afraid to bathe your dog. In books and publications I've read, many writers scoff at bathing, saying it will wash away the dog's natural oil, dry the skin, and so on. I don't believe it, and haven't had any problems from "overbathing" a dog. The statement is, in my opinion, ridiculous. A case in point: I have a mixed Alaskan Husky that is nothing less than part of the family. During the warm months, Max spends many hours outside doing what most dogs do, getting dirty. Some weeks she gets a shower with us every single night of the week before she is turned loose to roam the house. She has certainly suffered no ill effects from bathing. Her fur is soft, silky, and always smells sweet and fresh. The showers also make her feel good. During the toweling she pulls and plays and gets wound up for hours, the same as a person after a cool refreshing shower.

I'll agree Maximum gets bathed more than is usual for a dog. Unless my beagles get into some real nasty stuff they are bathed only once or twice a year, usually in the spring and again late in the summer. Bathing is a simple operation. Find a suitable container the dog will fit in, and fill it with warm water. I've used laundry sinks, metal tubs, cattle stock tanks, and anything that will do the job. My favorite is a large sloping wheelbarrow; it has plenty of room, holds lots of water, and is easy on the back.

There are plenty of good dog shampoos on the market, or you can use baby shampoo or something with coconut oil in it. Flea and tick shampoos are also available if these pests are giving you problems. You may want to plug the hound's ears with a little cotton and be sure to keep the shampoo out of his eyes. Get the dog wet and rub in the shampoo; then repeat the rubbing and wetting with the bath water several times. When he is clean, rinse well with a hose. You can towel dry him if you like, but in warm weather I simply let him shake all he wants and then put him back in a clean pen or tie him out in clean grass.

When the dog is almost dry, I spray him down with a mixture of Avon Skin-So-Soft and water. A 25 percent mixture (25 percent Skin-So-Soft and 75 percent water) in a small spray bottle will do it. The Skin-So-Soft replaces some skin oil, makes the coat, shine and also repels fleas and ticks. The Skin-So-Soft also makes the hound smell good. I stumbled across the Avon treatment by accident, and it does work well. We now use it as an insect repellent during spring turkey hunting. We understand that Avon was not too happy at first about people using their bath oil as insect repellent, but now market it as such. In any case, the Skin-So-Soft does work well as bath oil or insect repellent and is a good product for the dog owner.

Don't overlook brushing as another way of keeping your beagle clean and healthy. A beagle's hair requires a rather soft brush with a dense concentration of bristles. Brush the way the hair is going. You'll be amazed at how much dead and loose hair is removed. Brush as often as you can, especially after bathing and during the shedding seasons.

Keeping Other Pests in Check

While the dog is out of his kennel having his bath or drying, don't overlook his exercise area, feed and water pans, and his sleeping quarters. Give them all a good scrubbing with the hose and a little disinfectant. During the summer it is a good idea to remove any old bedding, as it is just a breeding ground for mites and other pests. If you've given your pet another place to stretch out, such as a sleeping bench, he'll spend a lot of time there instead of in the doghouse. Keep both clean and free of old rugs or hay.

When flies become a nuisance, we hose down the entire kennel and then spray the whole place, including the sleeping box, with a commercial insecticide. These are available at hardware, farm, and garden stores, are suitable for wiping on horses and cattle, and we've never known them to bother our dogs. We never spray or wipe the dog directly, but saturate the wood, wire, floor, everything with the insecticide using a small pump-type sprayer. The Avon Skin-So-Soft mixed about 50/50 this time is also great for spraying the sleeping areas and as well as the dog. When the dog is placed back in the pen, he'll also rub and scratch and naturally get some insecticide on himself. Occasionally, if we see live fleas, we will dust the dog with a regular flea powder. Dog owners are very fortunate today as they have an array of good products to help them fight off fleas, flies, and ticks.

As stated earlier, heading off problems before they start is better than dealing with them later. Cleanliness is truly the best way to ward off problems caused by fleas, flies, lice, and the hundreds of mites and other parasites that can live in your dog's kennel and sleeping area.

Removing Ticks

Ticks are a problem all over the country and as soon as the dog is placed in fields and high weeds he's going to pick up ticks. Ticks spread and carry all kind of diseases and should be removed as soon as they are discovered. Some people are scared to death when they encounter a tick gorged with blood. Actually this is a female tick, and it is not uncommon for a small male tick to be hanging onto her.

In most cases, it is a good idea to kill the tick before removal by painting it with alcohol or fingernail polish. However, if the tick is not too deeply imbedded, it can be pulled off by hand. Simply grip the tick as close to the skin as possible and pull with steady pressure until he breaks loose. If the head happens to come off and remains imbedded in the skin, it will not harm the dog. Apply an antiseptic to the area and the wound will scab over in a couple days. When the scab is removed or falls off, the head of the tick will come with it. If the dog is loaded with ticks, a commercial dip may be a better solution.

It does seem that ticks are not as severe a problem on beagles as they are on longer-haired dogs. The beagles' short, sleek hair gives him some protection, but ticks are still common in warm weather. Be alert for them. Get them off the dog immediately. During the warm summer months check the dog regularly for ticks, including the ears and the spaces between the toes.

Ticks and the Hounds

Several kinds of ticks can be bothersome to our beagles, the most common being the wood tick, the deer tick and the common brown dog tick. Although none of these are extreme nuisances, especially to those of us in the north, it's a good idea to check your hounds carefully after running in warm weather.

A host of diseases can be carried by various species of ticks including Canine Babesiosis (a blood disease affecting the spleen and liver), Rocky Mountain spotted fever, Q-fever, encephalitis, and tularemia (also associated with rabbits), and Lyme disease. All of these can infect our dogs in some way if they contact a tick carrying the sickness. Beagles are particularly easy to keep free of ticks because they are easy to spot on the short fur. A quick inspection after returning from the field is always advised.

Deer ticks are particularly worrisome because they are so small, barely the size of a pin head, and they are associated with Lyme disease. Lyme disease affects the dog much like it does humans; a weakened, flu-like sickness, followed by stiff and sore joints. Since dogs cannot tell us exactly what is bothering them it can be a difficult diagnosis, and a blood test is usually needed. Veterinarians can treat Lyme disease in dogs, but prevention is the best defense. If Lyme disease is prevalent in your area, there are drugs and topical insecticides that can be used as preventative measures.

As mentioned in the text, Avon Skin-So-Soft is a good product for keeping ticks and fleas from infecting the dogs, heading off problems. The Skin-So-Soft contains mostly fragrances, mineral, carrot and palm oil and a couple chemicals not usually harmful to man or beast. It doesn't contain the stronger insecticide DEET, but for some reason repels mosquitoes, ticks and fleas. I mix it about 50 - 50 with water and place it in a spray bottle or small garden sprayer. It can be applied directly onto the dogs and is routinely used to disinfect the sleeping quarters. During summer bath sessions I mix Skin-So-Soft 25% with 75% water.

Ticks are not difficult to remove and I commonly remove them just by pinching them off with the firm grasp of the fingers. Alcohol can then be applied to the site. Also, fingernail polish, alcohol, or even Vaseline can be applied to the live tick to kill it first before removal. Quick removal and keeping the dog away from tick infested areas is always a good idea. Ticks are not a giant problem for the hound owner but their notorious reputation for carrying a variety of illnesses should not be overlooked. The mere presence of ticks should ring an alarm bell for the dog owner . . . check for others, and always consider more serious repercussions if the dog comes down with anything.

Ear Problems

I have had a few dogs that had problems with their ears. Fluid, grass, or something getting in the ear and allowing bacteria to grow usually caused these problems, although in some cases tiny ear mites invaded the ears. After watching my vet many times, I began cleaning the dog's ears myself by flushing them with a warm, soapy solution, or diluted peroxide using a syringe (again, with no needle) or a clean plastic tube with a suction ball on the end. After treatment, rinse the ear out well with warm, clear water and let the dog shake. You may also want to add some mineral oil or antibiotic ointment to the ear. If the problem doesn't clear up in a few days, or you just don't think you can handle the procedure, see your vet.

Ear mites can be dealt with in much the same way, but after cleaning an insecticide must be placed in the ear. Usually, if both ears are infected and the dog shakes his head violently (a sure sign his ears are itching him), he likely has ear mites. Special creams and ointments are available to rid the dog of ear mites.

Some dogs are prone to reoccurring ear mite infestations, and a few of my dogs are routinely given a few drops of oil just to keep this ailment from becoming a problem. Ear mites are not a debilitating infection, but they can drive the dog crazy and cause other sores to develop from the dog constantly scratching. It is just another small problem that must be looked out for.

Eyes

For his entire life, my dog, Buster, had problems with his eyes because he didn't have enough tears to wash them. His eyes would glaze over and look terrible the morning after a hunt. Everyday before hunting I would have to flush and clean them, and I always carried a bottle of Visine or Clear-Aid in my hunting coat. He and I both learned to deal with the problem with a little cooperation on both sides. When he was young, I had him checked by my vet and the tear duct problem would have required an expensive operation. Had I known the dog was going to turn into a great hunter and spend his entire life with me, I would have spent the money and had his eye problem corrected.

When hunting heavily, weeds and pollen do irritate the beagles' eyes. Don't be afraid to look into the problem of removing any sticks or seeds the same way you would from your own eye. Flush the eyes with any good eye solution or plain water if you have nothing else. For scratched or very sore eyes keep a tube of terramycin ointment on hand. Squeeze a little in the infected eye for several days; the results are remarkable.

Feet and Pads

All this care is designed for really only one reason: to keep your dog healthy so he can give 100 percent while hunting. Since the beagle does all his work on his feet, it is not uncommon for him to suffer some injuries to these four parts of his body. Some bad cuts to legs and pads, as well as sprained legs and ankles, will require putting the dog up for weeks, even months, before he can hunt again. The recuperative powers of a dog are truly amazing, and they can recover from some pretty nasty injuries. I once had a dog that was rolled by a car while chasing a rabbit. The dog was busted up badly and had a dislocated shoulder. I lost her for the remainder of the season, but she hunted fine for years afterwards.

Minor foot problems can be corrected by the dog owner and can keep the dog hunting with a little effort. As stated previously, dogs kept on wire develop long toenails and must be clipped frequently. If not, the nails curve under and become long, sore, and a nuisance for the dog. The upper dewclaw nail will actually curve around and dig into the leg. Some dog breeders remove the dewclaws on all their pups shortly after birth.

Dogs may fight, kick and squirm during the procedure, but don't think for a minute they don't know who takes care of them. Here Ralphie reluctantly lets Dave dig a thorn out of his paw.

A vet will charge anywhere from $10 to $20 to clip nails, but it is not a difficult task, and the cost of a dog nail clipper is only a few dollars. If your dog has white nails, you can usually see where the live tissue stops growing. Even black nails can be trimmed easily once you get the feel of it. Start slowly and trim each nail a few times if necessary. Don't be afraid if you draw a little blood; just back off on the next nail, using this one as a guide. Be careful, but it is unlikely you're going to hurt the dog.

Make sure you get them all. This may sound silly but it is easy to miss one. The dewclaw, or fifth toe, is high up on the inside ankle of the front leg. Most dogs have only four toes on the hind legs, nature having done away with the fifth. I've also seen a few beagles that had six toes on each leg, and these were common on this particular strain.

When dogs are run hard day after day in tough thorny terrain, they're going to get thorns and briar spines in their feet. In our neck of the woods, large crabapple thorns are disastrous to my dogs. On the opening day of cottontail season one year, my dog, Berries, drove the three-inch spikes completely through three of her paws and had another embedded in the fourth. The dog was always oblivious to pain and continued to hunt, I might add.

During hunting season, when the dogs are hunted hard, I'm constantly picking thorns out of their pads and in between the toes. Sometimes I may have a needle handy, stashed in my hat or my coat collar somewhere. In some cases, depending on where I hunted that day, I may place each dog on an examination bench and check the paws with a strong flashlight. My wife, or a hunting buddy, holds down the dog while I check out each foot, digging out thorns with a needle as I go. In severe cases I may apply thimerosal (Merthiolate) or rub antiseptic cream into the wounds.

This isn't as big a project as it sounds. When in the field, I make a mental note of any dogs I see limping and which paw they are favoring. If I can't see anything while hunting, I'll check the paw under a light when I get home. I've also learned to feel/inspect all the dogs after each hunt. If the dog appears fine, I just run my fingers over the pads and in between the toes. You'll be surprised how easily you can detect thorns and cuts with a little practice. This saves time, especially when no help is available.

Another method I've used to protect feet and pads when I know I'm going to run the dogs hard for several days is the application of Tuf-Skin. Tuf-Skin is a product used by athletes as a base under tape. Tuf-Skin supposedly protects the skin and helps toughen soft tissue. Before each hunt, I place the dog on the truck tailgate and give each paw a liberal spraying of Tuf-Skin. He's then placed in the cage and the material dries on the way to the hunt. Some of the material does come off, but Tuf-Skin continues to build up with each application. Tuf-Skin is available at sporting-goods stores. I'm not sure how much this helps ward off cuts and thorns, but I'm after anything that will help (even if it is only a little) the dog make it through the season. Taking care of thorns and cuts quickly is worth the effort to keep your dogs hunting which is the ultimate goal.

Skin Problems

Have a dog long enough and you'll eventually have to deal with some kind of skin disease. Most of these are tied to cleanliness or nutrition in some way and can be dealt with, with a combination of improved diet, cleaner surroundings, a commercially prepared skin medicine, and common sense. The problem is identifying the multitude of diseases that may crop up. A self-cure is certainly feasible, but when in doubt consult the vet, especially if the dog doesn't show any noticeable improvement within several days.

Fortunately, I have been able to deal with all my beagle skin problems on my own. Most problems occurred in new dogs and pups that were gotten from someone else. The dogs were received with very dry skin, mange, or some other ailment already underway.

Each case of mange (mange is actually a name of a single ailment, but is now commonly used as a generic term for just about every dog skin problem) is judged and diagnosed as an individual. Some may be little more than eczema and can be treated by an application of a skin lotion.

When a dog begins to develop a coat that just doesn't look right, I may attack the problem from several angles. I worm the dog, give it some good quality canned food, add some type of oil or bacon grease to its dry food, disinfect the entire kennel, and bath and treat the specific area of infection. This may sound like overkill, but you want to stop the infection as quickly as possible, and one of these treatments usually does the trick when you are not sure just what is causing the skin problem.

Real honest-to-goodness mange is usually out of the reach of any home cure, as special insecticides and treatments are needed. See your veterinarian. Mange is caused by a tiny parasite that tunnels under the skin. This rascal is tough to kill, and in years past even the vet wrote the dog off. Today the parasite has been identified and new treatments are available that will rid the dog of this infestation. The actual parasite is a natural, common occurrence on almost all dogs and lives there all the time. It only becomes a problem when it gets out of control and starts burrowing under the skin.

The vet will take a scrapping of the infected area, and will even show you the little oval-shaped bug under the microscope. There are several different kinds of mange and the mites that cause the affliction, which is why it is best to seek out the expertise of a vet. Once identified, the vet will give special shampoos and insecticides to kill the mite causing the disease.

With all the ailments discussed so far, prevention is far better than fighting the problem once it has gained a beachhead. So it is with skin problems. Prevent most of them with good food, clean surroundings, and common sense.

As we said at the outset, this book was not intended to be a substitute for the services of a good veterinarian or even begin to cover the infinite number of ailments waiting to sneak up on your hunting partner. There are a couple of good books that deal with dog ailments and care and they cover each item in great detail, should the dog owner be interested in a more in-depth study. The ailments listed here are just some of the problems and general care items I've encountered and learned to deal with. It's not a tough job, and if I can do these things, I'm sure you can too. You'll find taking care of your beagle gives you added satisfaction, and will save you a lot of money. You'll also discover that you and the dog will develop a special bond of loyalty. He'll understand that you care about him and love him. He'll look to you when he's in trouble. He'll also return that love and loyalty when you go hunting–and that's all we can ask.

The beagle breeder must be careful and not breed just to see another litter of pups on the place. Breeding should be undertaken to improve the breed or to carry on traits from great dogs. Choose the parents wisely.

16

BREEDING YOUR BEAGLE

A t some point in time, a beagle owner may find himself in the situation where he wants to get puppies from a dog that has served him well. The only way to do that is to breed the dog and get offspring from it. This, the dog owner does, giving little regard to genetics or, in many cases, a simple family background check.

When I began this book, I thought this would be the most difficult chapter to write, as I figured an in-depth explanation of genetics, strains, conception, and breeding would be in order. I was wrong. For weeks, I pored over books on genetics and breeding of beagles only to discover much of the information was irrelevant or simply out of the realm of the average beagle owner or breeder. When a cottontail hunter finally has a dog he is in love with, he simply wants to have another like it, or wants to hold on to the memories that this particular dog provided

So, my first real advice on the breeding of beagles is to select your sire and bitch well. Is this dog that great and does it have so many good traits that it is worthy to carry on the beagle breed? Do you expect its pups to perform as good as the parents? Are you sure you won't get attached to these pups and be blinded by substandard performance just because they are the progeny of Old Duke. I can already see you nodding your head, so I won't talk you out of breeding a dog if you feel you must. I will say that the beagle breed has not been helped by the many owners who have bred dogs indiscriminately for a certain trait or simply to turn a nice profit on a batch of pups.

Taking this a step further, I can give a perfect example of dogs not to breed. More than 25 years ago, I started a red and white strain of beagles that have become excellent hunters. Many call these lemon and white and associate them with the well-known Patch Hounds, but in all honesty, they had no Patch relatives that I am aware of. I bred mostly for color and the fact that they are very mellow, well-mannered dogs. I only bred a few selected animals to get pups for my own use and sold or gave the excess pups to friends in the area. This is an example of close line breeding, keeping all breeding within the family. (There will be more on the types of breeding later.) But as my red-and-white strain became more and more known in my area, several guys brought their bitches to me to be bred with one of my red males. I never charged for this, but simply took a pup from the litter. Incidentally, this is an example of crossbreeding, breeding to an individual outside the family or strain. Each pup I received from these crosses showed many traits from my original dogs, and some became excellent hunters. They were, however, individuals, with their own quirks and characteristics not readily seen in my red-and-white line, and I never bred my red dogs back to any of them no matter how well they performed as individuals. Why?

In simple terms, I knew little or nothing about the background of the mother of these individual pups. Even though the pup itself may have been a good individual, it may have had skeletons in the closet, with undesirable traits that could surface in the next breeding. This is where years can be wasted in any breeding program. Also, breeding back to one of these pups would break or dilute the blood of my original strain, throwing many unknown factors into the formula. In effect, this crossbreeding would be starting another strain entirely. Training and environment are important, but they can never totally overcome the influences of heredity, or the inherited traits passed on from the parents.

Sure, beagle pups are cute and adorable, but some serious thought must be given to 'extra' pups and the time and effort that will be involved in seeing the puppies raised to adult hunters.

I would like to add here that this book was not intended as an encyclopedia on all aspects of beagling, and such is the case with this chapter on breeding. I would also add that there are several good books out there dealing specifically with the breeding of beagles, and anyone interested should consult all the material he can get his hands on. I do, however, feel that when a person buys a book dealing mostly with the hunting of beagles, he expects the writer to cover breeding in some way. And while I do not consider myself an expert on the subject, I do have some experience in the field. I have raised hundreds of puppies in my backyard kennel, and many have turned out to be exceptional gundogs. Somehow I was smart enough to know and keep one major rule in my breeding program: Keep it simple and don't mix blood. What I mean is that I kept things very basic; breeding my best individuals to get more pups for my own use, and never experimenting just to see another litter of puppies on the place. What I have practiced has been a combination of line breeding and at times some inbreeding. At present, I have ten dogs in my kennel. Nine of them are close relatives, and eight I raised from puppies.

The concept of line breeding, inbreeding, and crossbreeding is fuzzy to me. A beagle is a beagle. So how can we separate this family into hundreds of strains or lines? By breeding outstanding individuals to other outstanding individuals in hopes of getting something more outstanding. Also, in my opinion, the very best hounds have already been discovered, but senseless breeders kept breeding, not to improve the breed, but to "slow down," "speed up," or "make pretty" a particular batch of beagles. Do you see how all this breeding can become fuzzy? The point is, you wouldn't breed your beagle to a German shepherd so the pups would be bigger and have longer legs. You'd breed her perhaps to a slightly bigger beagle. So if it looks like a beagle, acts like a beagle, and runs rabbits like a beagle . . . it's probably a beagle, and you can bet he has a lot of common ancestors that you just don't know about. Refining certain traits or quelling bad ones is what breeding is really all about. Some breeders have done outstanding jobs; others have flooded the beagle breed with hundreds of mediocre, and in many cases unwanted, dogs.

In keeping with the theme of this chapter, Breeding Your Beagle, we'll give a brief description of the three types of breeding. Although two of them have already been mentioned, most beaglers are not familiar with the three types.

Inbreeding is the practice of breeding closely related animals. Although looked upon as some sort of taboo, inbreeding is a common practice among experienced breeders. In fact, as I have mentioned at length, when you think about it, no beagle can be purebred without having some inbreeding in its background. Many of today's hounds are related much more closely than the owners realize.

More beagle owners need to consider inbreeding instead of breeding to an animal they know little about. Inbreeding suggests a mating between close relatives such as father to daughter.

Line breeding is nothing more than another form of inbreeding. In line breeding, however, animals, in this case beagles, bred together are not as closely related as in inbreeding. An example of line breeding is breeding individuals further down the line, such as cousins, back to their great grandfather. The resulting puppies would have the same common ancestor or another close relative in their line. First and second cousins are commonly bred together in line breeding, but as you can see, the breeding is still within the same family of ancestors. Line breeding ensures good control over the breeding, usually with expected good results. In line breeding a strain or family can be bred for many years without outside influence. In reality, there is not a lot of difference between line breeding and inbreeding.

Outbreeding (sometimes called outcrossing or even crossbreeding) is the practice of breeding individuals that have no close common ancestors. As mentioned before, a true outcross breeding within the beagle species is nearly impossible. Outcrosses are commonly used to introduce a new trait into a strain or line, or give the strain new blood. It is believed that outcrosses give line-bred dogs new energy and strength.

Long into my breeding of the red-and-white strain, I ran out of good females to carry on the line. Since I am partial to females as hunters and my best male, Buster, proved a poor breeder, I slowly ran out of dogs to carry on the line. After a time, I discovered a red-and-white female beagle (again, many would consider these lemon and white) that was from good parentage and had many traits similar to my dogs. After hunting her for two seasons and studying her, an outcross between this bitch and my red/orange male, Ralphie (Buster's only living son) provided five outstanding pups and two that were extremely close in character to the original strain. These two, as well as the original female, were bred to keep the line going. Although the new genes have brought some different traits to the strain, the integrity of the original family is still somewhat intact. Without the outcross breeding, the line would probably have been headed for extinction in several more years. It should be noted again, however, that bringing any new individuals into the strain, even for one crossbreeding, actually begins a new strain even if only slight changes can be noticed. That is why each individual chosen for breeding should be carefully paired with its mate. In any kind of breeding–line, cross, or otherwise–the results are to secure pups that most closely resemble the parents in every way.

Let me reiterate that before you dive into any breeding program, or just begin

The author with Berries, the foundation for his breeding program. Berries' progeny are still running rabbits and continue to carry her traits many years after her death. When a hunter has a good dog, it is likely he will want offspring from it.

by breeding a single dog to get pups like Duke, choose the parents well, and save yourself years of heartache and frustration.

With everything that has been mentioned so far in mind, and after you have chosen two healthy individuals, free of any major diseases, it is a simple procedure to let nature take its course to get the bitch bred. Most female beagles come in heat roughly two times a year, four to six months apart, though others may come in heat only once a year. The heat cycle follows the weather and the amount of light available, and in my part of the world dogs usually come in heat in middle to late November and again in late March or April. Keep in mind, however, that a given female may come in heat anytime during the year. The estrus cycle will last somewhere around 20 days, and the female will usually stand and is receptive to the male during the middle of her cycle, at or about ten days.

It should go without saying that the bitch being bred should be kept isolated from any other dogs during this period. Since a litter of puppies is conceived through many egg cells, it is possible for the female to be bred and carry puppies by two different male dogs. I'll repeat that once again. It's possible for two puppies from the same litter to have different fathers, so it is important for contact to be limited to only the male you have chosen.

The two hounds should be given a quiet place, and the male will sometimes require a good solid floor of wood or concrete. In my above-ground kennels, I sometimes place a piece of carpeting or rough cardboard on the floor to give the male traction. The actual breeding where the dogs are locked together for some time will often happen at night, but some good breeding males take only a few minutes anytime of the day. Sometimes, if the dogs are very familiar with you, the male may require some help in mounting the bitch or holding her still. In most cases, however, the mating will take place on its own. I have read and heard that dogs do not have to accomplish the "tie" for the bitch to get bred, and this may or may not be true. The "tie," however, is the unmistakable sign that breeding has taken place, and once I see the dogs locked together, I remove the female. If you need help getting the actual mating accomplished, and some problems do come up, I suggest you consult a more in-depth book on breeding or see your vet.

All beagles are related in some way, although there are now many families and strains. Pictured here are Lightning and Annie Oakley.

Once the bitch is bred, and she is out of heat, she can return to her normal duties of hunting until the time of whelping is closer. That is not to say you should not pamper her slightly, and running her from daylight to dark would not be advisable. I have run bred females four or five hours a day throughout the hunting season and have had absolutely no problems. As the pregnancy develops and the dog becomes bigger and the teats begin to hang and get torn and damaged, it is time to put the dog up and wait for the pups to be born.

Throughout the pregnancy the bred female should be fed a good quality diet. Many feeds are designed for brood bitches and will help her obtain a better volume of milk. If the dog is healthy and fed a good quality food, I see no reason to change from her normal diet. I simply add a few cans of moist dog food from time to time and save some choice table scraps for her.

It is also important that the bitch be free of worms before she gives birth. Worms thrive on mother's milk and in the intestines of newborn puppies, and can quickly kill the pups. Worm the bred bitch a couple weeks after mating and again a couple weeks before the pups are born. The chemicals will pass from the mother directly into the pups and they will, in most cases, be born free of worms. I cannot stress enough the importance of this one item of care, as it seems that many neglect it. This problem is so easy to avoid. If the puppies are born full of worms, you've got a serious problem on your hands that only a vet can help you with, and it is a very good bet some of the litter will die. Although I've never had any problem with worms after worming the dam, some worm species can survive and be transferred to the puppies, so watch them carefully. Puppies having a round potbelly and dull, lack-luster coat could be infected with round worms. The whole litter should be treated at about three weeks or even earlier should you see or suspect a worm infestation.

The gestation period of dogs is between 60 and 75 days, with bigger breeds often carrying puppies longer. Beagles will have their pups between 62 and 65 days from the time of mating. There is little you need to do if everything has developed normally. If the mother dog is used to being outside, then leave her there, providing she has a clean, comfortable, warm box. Provide her with clean fresh hay, old sheets or rags, and, in cold weather, a small light bulb (25 watt or 40 covered) may be hung in the box for additional warmth. Sometimes a special whelping box can be built, and how extensive you get with this is up to the breeder. Some bitches will inadvertently lie on a few pups, and sometimes I will fasten a three-inch wide board along the wall of the box a few inches from the floor. This will give the pups

A typical whelping box with raised floor section and wind panel to keep air from entrance hole blowing directly on puppies. Notice the covered light on wall for cold nights and the first few days after birth.

The nesting box looks much like any other dog house and can be used as such other times. The entire roof lifts off for cleaning and access to pups.

somewhere to squirm away from an anxious mother. The boards work well protecting pups and can be removed after a week or so.

Other than that, your new mother hound will do just fine without any help from you. Of course, if the hound gets down for more than a few hours without any signs of puppies or anything that does not seem normal, a vet should be contacted if only for advise and piece of mind. In most cases, this will be unnecessary, but I always have my vet's number handy and have even alerted him early when I have expected trouble.

The new beagle mother will have anywhere from one to five puppies. The normal litter for a beagle the second time around is seven. Litters of ten or eleven are not uncommon, but are not the norm. Most of the time the pups will be roughly the same size, and there may or may not be a runt of the litter.

Although there is little the dog owner has to do for the first few weeks, common sense should again prevail. If it has been a messy birth, don't be afraid to wrap all the pups in warm towels, remove them, and change the hay or bedding in the whelping box. I've always used fresh, sweet-smelling hay for the whelping box, and the mother dog seems to prefer this over most other bedding. Inside my barn kennel, where I can watch the birth closely, I clean up blood and fluids as quickly as possible, and change the bedding as the mother allows me. I have also raised pups inside my barn kennel with no bedding, simply adding a fiberglass heating-pad to the wooden floor of the box. These heating pads work great, can be adjusted for low or high heat, and again help the pups develop rapidly.

If the dog is kept outside and used to the cold, I prefer to leave them there. In extremely harsh weather, I may tape a thermometer to the inside of the box and check it several times a day, and during the night. It's good if the box can maintain a temperature from 70° to 85°F (aided by the small light bulb). The mother will provide additional warmth to about 95°F. I once raised a litter of five pups outside in March, in weather that was −10°F. Of course, I watched them closely, and checked on them throughout the night. The pups and the mother were doing so well that I saw little reason to bring them inside. In a few days, the weather broke, and I slept just fine! Little things such as this take some of the pressure from the mother and help speed up the development of the pups. The first three days are the most critical time, and once the pups cross this threshold, their chances of survival soar.

Caring for the Pups

Since you've entrusted the future of your hunting on this mating and litter of puppies, you want to do everything you can to see that every pup makes it to a point in their life where you can evaluate their potential. In 30 years and countless breedings, I have lost only a few puppies; most were rolled on by a careless mother, although one was killed by parvo-virus at 12 weeks of age, before vaccine could fully protect it. Some of the pups I've raised–like Buster and Ralphie, Lightning, Sammy and Storm–turned into exceptional dogs and actually kept me in hunting dogs and the strain going for years. I shudder to think what would have happened if I had been careless and lost them when they were infants. Every pup is important. Their potential may not be known for months or even years down the road, but every one is important.

Sue-Sue at six weeks of age. You may have entrusted the future of your rabbit hunting to a specific breeding. Each pup's potential may not be known for months or even years, but every pup is important.

In nine or ten days the puppies will open their eyes and start crawling around. They will fall out of the box and generally start getting antsy. This is an important time for the puppy and for the owner. It is the first time in his life the pup will see humans and see that, besides his mother, you provide all of his other needs. It is at this time that a strong bond can develop between the pups and their new master. In some particular pups this bond will become extremely strong and will last for their entire lives should the breeder decide to keep them. This special bond of friendship and loyalty will help both the hunter and the dog develop into a remarkable hunting team. I have always contended that a puppy raised and trained by the person who will hunt and work the animal is far better than a hound that is bought and sold and has many owners throughout its life. I have very special feelings for the dogs that I have raised from puppies and turned into good hunters, and who have lived their entire lives with me. You can see and feel that special bond between them and me every day when I go to the pens, or on every hunt.

At about three or four weeks of age the young dogs will be receptive to licking your fingers and searching out water. Here again, the dog owner can strengthen the bond between him and the litter by handling the pups and encouraging them to drink water. Soon the pups will be ready to mouth and suck on soft food, and are well on their way to being weaned.

Within five weeks, the mother's duties are almost over, although if kept with the pups she may allow them to suck for several more weeks. This is not harmful and actually helps to dry up the bitch's milk. In any case, all the puppies will be weaned between six and nine weeks of age. Puppies being sold or given to friends can go to their new homes when they are between six and eight weeks old. If everything has progressed smoothly, you now have several new beagles that are full of energy and the hope of the new owner.

Breeding your beagle is not particularly difficult, but carries with it a fairly big responsibility. Both the mother and the litter require care and attention. Few of us can raise and train an entire litter, so some thought must be given to the excess pups. It's a good idea to have potential homes for them way before they are even born. Many breeders destroy unwanted pups, but that is difficult. The novice breeder must realize that he's going to have his hands full with five or six "extra" pups, and should give serious thought to their fates before they are even born.

The breeder must also realize that the new pups will be total novices at hunting, and months, even years, will be required before they are the finished, experienced hunters he expected. The step from simple dog owner to dog breeder must be taken carefully and with thought to the consequences.

The special bond of friendship and loyalty helps both the hunter and the dog develop into a remarkable hunting team.

Pursuing Mr. Cottontail with a video camera and crew was much more involved and complicated than I anticipated.

17

THE FIRST RABBIT VIDEOS

Did you ever do something so much, that at some point it started to become boring or just didn't hold the luster that you once saw in it? So it was with rabbit hunting for me during the early 1980s. Looking back, I can see it was a combination of things. I had lost my old and reliable dog, Berries, and the rabbit population had fallen off at the same time. A new pack leader was slow in emerging from the small, motley group of young dogs I had, and it seemed like it didn't matter whether I went bunny hunting or not.

About this time, a friend and acquaintance from Dubois, Pennsylvania, came out with his first video on turkey hunting. The market was hungry for this type of video back then, and his tape was a great success. I talked to Denny Gulvas about his production several times, and about the idea I had of making a cottontail hunting video. Denny encouraged me to follow through with the idea, but an independently produced video was a big gamble, and certain to be expensive.

After pondering and discussing the idea for almost two years, I decided to go ahead with the project. I'll never forget the day my wife walked in and I quietly announced I was taking all of our $6,000 in savings and going to make a videotape on rabbit hunting!

Linda never paused for a moment, but simply said, "Whatever you think, Hon."

With support like that it was hard to back away, and LinDavid Productions was born. The title of the tape would be easy; we would simply call it *Cottontail Rabbit Hunting*. In the weeks following, I jumped into the project head first, and quickly got the lesson of my life!

Since I had written many articles for newspapers and national magazines, writing a script and outline to follow was not a big problem. After many, many hours at the computer, I believed I had the rough outline of a 90-minute video.

I also knew that some scenes would have to be rewritten, and others added or dropped as actual production began.

During the pre-production stage, I also began work on designing a layout of the video box cover. I came up with a couple different ideas, wrote text to fit the spaces, and left openings for the color pictures we would add later. Months of work and time meeting with printers followed all through the actual work on the video.

The biggest problem was finding a cameraman willing to devote a lot of time outdoors in bad weather and still be reasonable enough so that we could see the project through to completion. Regular video production companies wanted as much as $500 a day. We placed ads in the local newspapers and several outdoor magazines. After a long and tedious task of interviews and groping around in the dark, I settled on a young man who had some experience, some equipment, and a whole lot of positive attitude! Mark Andrews turned out to be my biggest asset in seeing the tape through to the end, but he also became my biggest headache.

Mark would forget batteries, let equipment repairs go until things went down on a rabbit hunt two miles from the truck, show up unprepared, and generally took little interest in the project besides wondering when he was going to be paid. Yet, at the same time, Mark was energetic, eager to capture rabbits on film, and a great guy to work with. He wanted with all his heart to do a good job, but lacked experience and grown-up knowledge. Although there were times when I could have easily strangled him, through it all we became, if not good friends, at least friends.

Through the early fall we struggled through the stand-ups, the talking segments needed to introduce a hunt or explain some information. It was tough going. Equipment kept breaking. Airplanes, cows, cars, something would interfere with otherwise good "takes." Bright sun and bad weather would force us to shut down with barely anything accomplished, after planning and organizing shoots for days.

The money dwindled. To keep things moving, I bought extra VCR decks, cords, wire, videotape, and an endless supply of batteries. After several thousand dollars had been expended and countless hours of failures recorded, I seriously considered cutting my losses and giving up. But, of course, I didn't, and we struggled on. I borrowed more money. I was convinced a rabbit hunting film would sell, if I could ever get it finished!

When the actual hunting began, I became more at ease. Mark had bought a better camera and devised a system for wearing the microphone on his head. It was crude, but it worked. We slowly started to gather some pretty decent film and some actual rabbit kills on video. It was a grueling schedule. We hunted every day possible. Mark spent time charging batteries and keeping equipment clean and running at night, plus worked another job in Pittsburgh each morning. I worked on the box cover, ran to the printer, cared for the dogs, and rewrote scenes and organized shoots for stand-ups not yet filmed. It was a seven-day-a-week, no-pay, never-ending job. Even the dogs, which were called upon to run rabbits every day, began to tire.

Later in the Pennsylvania rabbit season, we were hunting on a particularly bad snowy and windy day. As usual, things weren't going real well, and with a bitter winter storm moving in, I knew we would have to return to the truck soon. Suddenly we shot one rabbit, and the dogs jumped another. They stayed on the trail well, and the rabbit circled at least twice. Finally, the bunny dove onto the snow-covered trail in front of us and came straight for the camera. I wanted desperately to hit the bunny up front so he would tumble for the camera, and fired a foot or so in front of him. Although definitely hit, he kept coming. The second shot did exactly what had been expected from the first, but added even more excitement and realism to the scene. It was a spectacular shot, and the one people always mention when they talk about the video. It was the one we had been waiting for all season, and in my opinion was the signature shot of *Cottontail Rabbit Hunting*.

The season ended in late January, and we were still filming stand-ups and scenes for credits that should have been done months earlier, but somehow it all got done. In early March, I walked into an editing studio in Pittsburgh, carrying a suitcase of videotape and 57 hours of rabbit hunting video.

The editing began as everything else had, slow and difficult. Bill, the editor, although not a hunter, fought me every step of the way for the first day or so. He came up with some great ideas and was a whiz at working the machinery, but he wanted to turn the tape into something totally different from what I had planned.

Is he right? I kept asking myself.

Finally, after several more arguments and disagreements on how the tape was supposed to proceed, I came to the conclusion that Bill had not been with the project for almost a year as I had. Also, he was not a hunter, and I felt I was much more capable deciding what rabbit hunters would want to see on a rabbit hunting video. Besides, I was paying the bill! Bill finally relented, and although he continued to offer excellent suggestions for transitions, graphics, and credits, we followed, almost to the letter, the outline I had taken months to put together.

The editing lasted almost a week. At $80 an hour, the money again slipped away. By the time the tape was finished, a three-minute demo tape was made, and the first 100 copies were in our hands, several thousand more dollars had vanished. But the excitement of finally seeing a finished product after a year of hard work helped take away much of the sting of all we had spent.

With the tape done, I pushed the printers and practically slept there overseeing the final printing of the art for the covers. During the editing stage, I had also been working on ads for several of the smaller outdoors and hound magazines. The ads were to run beginning with the April issues. In late March the tape was totally finished and 100 copies were stacked on my desk in the basement. I left town and went on a planned turkey hunt to Florida.

The video, now finished, was like a giant weight lifted from my shoulders. I got lucky. On the second day hunting in the swamps of Florida, I shot a nice adult spring gobbler. Naturally, I called home.

"Hey!" Linda yelled, "We got three orders for the rabbit tape in the mail today!"

"You're kidding!" I said. It was a strange feeling. All the work was done with the idea that we could sell a rabbit hunting video, but now that the first orders had come in, it seemed unbelievable.

As the summer passed and the leaves once again turned to the brilliant colors signaling another hunting season to come, the video orders came more frequently. With Christmas and winter "video weather," we slowly recouped all the money we spent and later went on to turn a nice profit. What's more is that hunters seemed to really like the video. Letters, cards, and telephone calls came from all over the country. This seemed to make up for the countless hours and days and months of frustration. They liked the video! I guess that is all we could have hoped for. Some of the hunters and beaglers I have met through the video will remain friends for the rest of my life. This was truly a fringe benefit I could never have predicted.

I don't think anyone could ever realize how much time, effort, money, and tears Linda and I put into that first video, *Cottontail Rabbit Hunting*. Beyond the idea of making a video for profit was the fact that we had begun something very difficult, with no real experience, and had seen it through to completion. At the end, it became an obsession to me. I think at one point, I didn't care if I ever made a dime on it, but . . . "I was finishin' the sucker!"

Also, because I ate, slept, thought, filmed, and hunted nothing but rabbits for a solid year, my interest in bunny hunting had truly been renewed. Now, I don't think a single day goes by that I don't talk about dogs or rabbit hunting to someone. All this came about because one day in 1987, I decided to make a rabbit hunting video.

The Others

They say, "Experience is the best teacher," and with *Cottontail Rabbit Hunting* under our belt, we decided to give the video game another try. A bit more ambitious this time, our plans were to make two videos at almost the same time.

The first thing I did was, of course, borrow more money. I wanted more of my own equipment this time around, and also wanted to maintain better picture quality of the finished tapes. The new tapes were shot in the newer Super-VHS format and bumped directly to one-inch tape. This kept the copies clean and crystal clear. Also, with newer, better equipment and wireless microphones, breakdowns were less common and things went smoother. Sure, it was still a tremendous amount of work, and juggling scripts, shooting stand-ups, and gathering footage for two separate videos kept me again working almost night and day.

The video, *Mostly Squirrels*, had to be shot almost entirely during the few weeks of colorful foliage to make the tape realistic. Mark again filmed some, but now I had trained myself in the use of the camera and the other aspects that go along with it. This meant that I could gather squirrel footage on my own, do stand-ups with the host, and film friends on actual squirrel hunts.

Capturing squirrels dangling high in the treetops, however, took a special knack and skill that no one but a hunter seemed to possess. This meant that I was forced to spend almost all the time behind the camera, and even then it was difficult to get the shots I was looking for. Weeks were spent filming hunts to get the few we would eventually use for the completed video. A squirrel video, what seemed at first should be much easier to put together than any rabbit tape, proved to be much more difficult.

With rabbit season already underway in Pennsylvania, I traveled to Indiana to film the squirrel dog segment planned for *Mostly Squirrels* with Allan Willsey, an avid squirrel dog hunter I had met when *Cottontail Rabbit Hunting* was released. The hunts went well and I returned home with some excellent footage, and one shot of a squirrel falling into the river that I knew would be the hit of the video. *Mostly Squirrels* was now shoved onto the shelf and we began filming and gathering footage for the second tape, *Cottontails & Hares*. The squirrel tape would not be edited or finished until the rabbit hunts were filmed.

While all this was going on, I was again designing covers for the video boxes. I worked with a printer closer to home, and things went somewhat better. When not hunting, we also filmed stand-ups with the two different hosts that did the talking parts and narration for each tape.

In December of 1990 my friend Bill Morgan and I headed to upstate New York to film the hare hunts with Zef Selca and some of his close relatives. It was a grueling five-day affair.

Zef Selca with his first Swiss hounds, Chica and Dexey. Zef was so nervous and tried so hard to help make the video, *Cottontails & Hares,* a success, he made filming difficult. However, his dedication to the project and his contribution of dogs and time were appreciated, and I truly thank him!

Zef, wanting things to go well, tried too hard, was very nervous on tape, and was so difficult to work with that he put everyone on edge. Somehow we managed to get some useable footage, but things were still tense. I finally had a talk with Zef.

"Zef," I said, "you've got to loosen up a little, quit bossing all the guys around and just let them hunt. Also, let the rabbits get out where we can see them and get them on film. Let's just hunt like we always do tomorrow, and forget about the camera. Let's just hunt!"

The next day things went better. Zef, although still jittery, had calmed down some and began to act more naturally. The rabbits, both hares and cottontails, were out and the guys killed several almost on cue. Several exciting misses also made the hunt more realistic. I now had enough hare footage to add a half-hour section to the video. In Zef's defense, it should be mentioned that it's different hunting in front of the camera when everything you do and say is being recorded. If you don't think so, just have someone follow you around all day on a hunt recording every single thing you do and say . . . anyone would be nervous. Zef Selca did his very best to help make *Cottontails & Hares* a success, and I truly thank him.

When hunting season was finally over, we spent the next few weeks in a new studio in Pittsburgh. We went back and finished the squirrel tape, then proceeded on to *Cottontails & Hares*. I was pleased with both of them, but really proud of *Cottontails & Hares*. I'm not sure why I favored the new rabbit tape over the squirrel, but believe it was because a rabbit tape had begun all this, and I felt the new tape was a big improvement over *Cottontail Rabbit Hunting*, filmed almost three years earlier.

I would like to say that both new tapes were as successful as the original, but at this time I can't. The time was right for *Cottontail Rabbit Hunting*, and I'm not sure if sales of the other two will ever catch up to it. Would I ever do it again?

Well, yes. After a short rest, I jumped in with both feet again and made the video, *Cottontails Again!*–completing the rabbit hunting trilogy. The tape came out very well and was another big success, but the project so drained me I swore I'd never make another one—something I had said each time out! And now I can't honestly say one way or the other, but I believe my video career is over. I'd also like to say the videos made me rich, but I can't do that either. I certainly didn't lose any money, and I continue to make a small profit as each tape sells. The real payment was in the experience I gained from doing something like this, and in some of the people I met along the way.

We had come up with an idea to make a few videos for sale, and somehow pulled it off having little or no experience, and the videos were good, and well received. It was incredible. I mean here I was out in the woods hunting with my dogs, working my butt off, and loving every minute of it. And if I juggle the figures around enough, I can actually say I was getting paid for it the whole time!

Bill Morgan (left) and Zef Selca stop long enough to pose for one quick picture during the filming of _Cottontails & Hares._

18

THE MYSTERY IN LAUREL SWAMP

Laurel Swamp: a strange foreboding place, certainly one of the strangest places I ever hunted. With six inches of fresh snow and heavy frost covering everything, the swamp took on the appearance of a living creature with arms and legs spreading out in all directions. The air around the swamp was slowly warming, and a soft mist of fog gave the frozen bottomland even more of an eerie appearance, enveloping the area with a feeling of mystery. Yet, Laurel Swamp held plenty of cottontails, and where there are cottontails you'd find the beagles and me.

This was my second trip to the swamp. The first time, falling snow had made the conditions so bad that it was hard to see any rabbits pushed out onto the swamp edge by the dogs. Still, the beagles barely stopped barking the whole time they were in there, and we just knew we'd have to try it again later. Today was the day.

Brian Salley and I led the dogs directly into the lower lip of the swamp, and in just a few minutes the dogs had started a rabbit. The marsh was barely 100 yards wide at this end, and the dogs quickly swung around it and were coming back to open woods. Aside from all the barking, you could hear ice snapping and popping under the weight of the four-dog pack. The hounds weren't falling through the ice, but it continued to crack and shatter as they ran over it.

"He's in the open woods!" Brian shouted.

I took a few steps toward him, but then the noise indicated that the dogs had turned away from the swamp. The dogs were having a tough time in the deep snow, but were staying with the track. About ten minutes later, Brian's gun went off and Laurel Swamp had given up its first rabbit of the day.

"There was another one sitting in the open woods," Brian reported. "I'm not sure which one I shot, but the other one went down that strip of brush there and back into the swamp."

We showed the hounds the fallen bunny and then ushered them down the strip where Brian had seen the other cottontail. They immediately picked up the trail and tore off back into the frozen wasteland of the marsh. It was too thick in there to follow or to do any serious shooting, so the only sensible plan was to simply wait until the dogs pushed the rabbits to the swamp edge or out into the open woods.

I went back to my original position 100 yards west of Brian. The swamp was its narrowest here, and the dogs had already come through this small neck. They were back in the open woods about 150 yards away and in plain view. I watched them swishing this way for 20 yards or so, then that way for 20 yards or so, to no avail. They appeared to have lost the trail.

The open hardwood forest was barren of any cover and they might as well have been searching for the cottontail on the fairway of any close-clipped golf course. "There's no way that bunny's lying there in the middle of all those dogs," I thought. Wrong! The dogs all screamed suddenly, and the bunny came up out of the snow like a brown missile! He covered the first 100 yards in fractions of a second and easily pulled away from the pursuing pack. I'm not sure if the rabbit saw me, but he made a shallow turn to the right and was now clear of the dogs. My shot intercepted him about 30 yards out and sent him plowing snow for another 15 feet. The dogs were on him before I could pick up the spent casing, and Lightning and Meg were having "discussions" on who was going to carry the bunny over to me. The whole incident was over in four seconds.

"Hey, that's great!" Brian shouted, arriving on the scene and reaching for his camera. "Don't know why those rabbits are leaving the swamp and coming into these open woods," he said, "but we've got lots more swamp ahead of us and I'm sure we'll get a few more."

The dogs ran a couple more bunnies at the small end of the swamp, but we were never in range when they were pushed in or out of the heavy cover. We decided to try the big end, where all the dense mountain laurel grew.

Having hunted Laurel Swamp for nearly 20 years, Brian knew it well and took the lead. As we entered the laurel, though, I was slightly disappointed. The rabbit sign was considerably less than we had seen earlier, and I was thinking that maybe we should have stayed in the lower end. Brian, undaunted, kept pushing deeper into the laurel. Finally we came upon a frozen pool covered by cottontail tracks.

"Ah, here's where they're living today!" he said triumphantly. "I'll swing around and get up by the road in case the dogs head that way." I didn't answer, but could hear the traffic on the road several hundred yards ahead, straight east. I watched Brian pick his way around the edge of the pool, his boots occasionally breaking through the ice. I think he could feel I was concerned. "These pools aren't too deep," he called back, "just stay on the edge or where the plants are growing."

The place gave me the creeps: an impenetrable barrier of laurel in all directions, ice and water all around me, and the hum of traffic not far enough away for my liking. The dogs could be on that road before we could get to them. The air was warmer now, but with all the snow and ice around I was actually chilly. Once in a while the soft mist would rise up from the ice and swirl around in the breezes.

"What a weird place!" I said to myself, shivering.

Lightning's sharp howl snapped me back to reality and the fact that we were supposed to be hunting. Annie Oakley cut in, and then came Ralphie's coarse chop–chop, telling us they had found a hot bunny. I stepped up onto a small mound of earth and listened intently to the chase. The dogs were hot and tearing through the laurel toward the north, away from the road. I breathed a small sign of relief and continued listening. They were turning now, heading in the general direction of the frozen pool I was watching. Must be one of the rabbits that left all these tracks, I reasoned.

The chase was coming straight for me now, and from Meg's excited squeal I knew the rabbit must be very close in front of them. Where is he? Why can't I see him? The dogs got right to the edge of the pool, just three or four feet inside the laurel, and turned sharply left. Why didn't he come across there? Did he see me?

I didn't have time to think much about it. The dogs barely went 40 yards and turned around again. They were coming back on almost the exact line they had just come down. Suddenly there's the cottontail! One more leap and he'll be on the ice . . . pointblank range. Using the heavy laurel to break some of the pattern, I fired almost directly at the bunny. I didn't see him go down, but he never jumped onto the ice. He was there, lying just a few feet inside the evergreen jungle of laurel. I scooped him up before the dogs could do anymore damage to him. He was in beautiful condition, hit only forward of the front legs.

Brian came up behind me and congratulated me on my 58th rabbit of the season. "Hey, those dogs are doing great. I'll bet we're going to get some more in here. We're right on schedule," he said noting the time. "There are tracks everywhere above this pool."

He was right, the place had some bunnies in it, and I was sure the dogs could push them out of the laurel. As I field-dressed the cottontail, the dogs started barking again.

"See, I told you," Brian said, as he sloshed around the pool again, breaking more holes so that the water slowly creeped up onto the ice. A few seconds later he was swallowed by a misty hole in the otherwise solid mass of green and white. I shook my head at the eeriness of the whole scene and hurried my cleaning. The dogs were heading northeast again, and I was confident they were going to follow the same general pattern.

"This is going too well," I thought. "It's just too easy." That's when everything fell apart.

I took a few steps and was back on the small mound of dirt from where I had shot the first cottontail. The dogs had already swung around and were coming on an angle straight for the pool where I was waiting. They couldn't have been more than 100 yards out through extremely thick cover. I could hear the patches of ice breaking under the weight of the four beagles; having raised each of them from puppies, I knew each voice clearly. Then, almost in mid-bark, Ralphie let out a blood-curdling scream, followed by a series of pain-filled yelps and barks. Something had hit or grabbed him! My heart jumped into high gear as Lightning also started to scream. I ran across the pool and desperately tried to find a way through the tangle of laurel and thick rhododendron. I was 30 yards from the pool and could make no more progress.

Suddenly, Ralphie was at my feet. There was blood all over the snow. My heart sunk.

"What's the matter, Ralph?" I asked gently. Ralphie retreated into the bushes a few yards, and then came back at my coaxing. I could see at least two major holes; blood was gushing from them, and running down his legs and onto the snow. I leashed him and made my way back to the open pool.

The wounds were perfect holes, pencil-sized. The dog had so much blood on his left front shoulder that I couldn't tell how badly he was hurt. There was also blood on his back and another wound on the opposite side of his neck. What could have done this to a dog so quickly? And where was Lightning? The wounds were so symmetrical that a .22 could have made them. Who could be up in there? With all the barking and ice cracking, could I have missed the sounds of a .22 barely 100 yards away?

"Brian!!"

From somewhere in the jungle Brian answers. "Yeah!"

"Can you get over here?"

He picked his way around the pool until he found me in an opening at the swamp edge. I was still trying to figure out how badly Ralph was hurt.

"Something's happened to the dog," I said. "He's been shot or something."

By the sound of my voice, Brian knew I wasn't kidding. We both examined the dog. The two holes I was most concerned about were in the front shoulder and directly behind and into the ribs. I shoved my small finger into the rib hole, partly trying to stop the blood and also trying to find out how deep it was. Ralphie, although scared, didn't look weak or out of breathe.

"I don't think his lungs are broken, but he's losing a lot of blood. We've got to get him out of here," I said to Brian. "Can you go for my truck while I try to round up the other dogs?"

"Yeah, but it's going to take me a while," he replied. The truck was completely on the other end of Laurel Swamp, a good mile and a half away. We hadn't expected to circle back to it until much later that afternoon.

"I know, just do the best you can. I'll get the dogs and lead them all out to the road." With that, Brian took off back along the edge of the swamp the way we had come in.

The other three dogs were still on the rabbit's trail, and I could easily hear Lightning. With her still on the trail and barking, I was pretty sure she was unhurt. She apparently had seen whatever happened to Ralphie, and had let out the screams from sheer terror. Now that she was back with Annie running, I felt better. I just had to get them out of there somehow.

I could hear the dogs coming toward me again, so I quickly tied Ralphie's leash to a tree and ran back to the pool as the dogs crossed the upper end. My screaming and yelling didn't turn them, and I knew Annie was not going to give up on a hot rabbit.

A quick check on Ralph and I headed back around the swamp edge and listened. The dogs had swung around again and were heading back into the area where Ralphie had been attacked. I had to get in front of them.

I slammed two shells into my 1100 and took off. If I could shoot the rabbit my troubles would be partly over. When I broke into a long opening, I could see that the dogs were coming straight for me!

I grabbed Annie first and held on. Lightning went down on her belly when I yelled at her, and I quickly snatched her collar. I was pretty sure Meg would not continue the chase on her own. Now that I had the dogs, I realized that two leashes were back with Ralphie.

The dogs were fighting to get loose. "Stay still!" I told them sternly. "We're in trouble here!"

I unclipped my gun sling and somehow got it under Lightning's collar and then Annie's. Lightning appeared to have no wounds or blood on her. With a whole lot of forcing and pleading, I slowly fought my way back to Ralph.

I was still clawing my way the last few yards out of Laurel Swamp when I saw the truck pull in to a nearby driveway. I was surprised Brian had made it back so soon, but then again, I had lost all track of time.

"I had the guy in the house there call the vet and tell him we were coming!" Brian shouted.

We hustled the three other dogs into the truck, and I carefully lifted Ralph onto the tailgate. We tore off for the 30-mile trip into Indiana, Pennsylvania.

X-rays revealed no metal fragments or bullets inside Ralphie, and the vet could not determine what had happened to him or what had made the perfect holes. Besides the wounds in the right neck, left front shoulder, and left rib cage, there were also two holes in the top of the back. Later, we also discovered that Lightning had been hit once below the left eye by the same strange attacker. The wound was the same perfect oval shape and matched Ralphie's wounds exactly. The entire attack had taken no more than ten seconds.

"What could have done that to a dog?" I questioned.

The vet just shook his head.

The good news was that Ralphie would recover. He was weak from loss of blood and his front shoulder was stiff and sore, but a couple weeks later he was back chasing rabbits.

Brian and I spent what little daylight was left back at Laurel Swamp investigating the incident. We circled the entire area and found no unusual tracks. There was no wire, fencing, or any man-made objects in the swamp. The rhododendron and laurel was so thick in the immediate area of the actual attack that we couldn't even get in there. As we walked back to the truck, Brian and I both expressed our dismay that we would never know what had happened to the hounds while coming up through the swamp.

"Well, something certainly reached up out of that swamp and grabbed a hold of them. I think that's pretty certain," I declared. "The Creature of Laurel Swamp, that's all I know."

Brian gave a soft laugh.

As we neared the truck I sneaked one last look back at the swamp. The mist and fog was slowly enveloping it and its secrets for another night.

Addendum After weighing all the evidence; the shape of the wounds, the fact that no other tracks came out of the swamp, the quickness of the actual attack, and several other factors, it was concluded that the dogs had probably been attacked by a large raptorial bird, possibly a large hawk, eagle, or owl. It is my opinion that the bird saw the cottontail and tried to intercept it, or that the bird was either feeding or injured on the ground when the dogs surprised it. A large owl would be the most logical candidate for this area, but again, we will never know what really happened to dogs coming through Laurel Swamp.

19

THOSE SPECIAL MOMENTS

Everyone can remember special moments that happened while hunting, moments that to anyone else would be meaningless. To a hunter, these are special slices of time, frozen in a picture, perhaps, or images stored away in a memory bank. For many it was the experience of taking their first deer, first wild turkey, and first rabbit, or perhaps watching their son on his first hunt. To others, it was the vision of that new pup, after months of hard work, circling his very first rabbit.

I have been blessed with so many great and memorable moments while hunting that it boggles my mind when I try to remember them all. Moments like sitting on the prairie in Oklahoma one afternoon and watching a thunderstorm rolling across the sage, thunder and lightning crackling all around; at the sound of each thunderclap, several nearby Rio Grande turkeys would gobble back their own kind of thunder. It is etched into my mind so vividly that it's almost as if it happened yesterday. Or, after hunting for several grueling weeks, I'm suddenly kneeling beside a huge Pennsylvania gobbler that came to my call after just five minutes in a pouring rainstorm. There's the picture of the time when I rolled my first pure-white snowshoe hare while hunting with Zef Selca in beautiful upstate New York. And rabbit hunts that yielded ten straight cottontails with ten shots, and my head was so big my hat kept falling off and I thought I might never miss another rabbit, only to get skunked the next day! Then there's the misty morning I dropped four running fox squirrels from a single tree with four shots. As I said, the memories come flooding back so strong they get cluttered in a kaleidoscope of changing patterns and color, enough to fill this entire book.

The 1991 season was just such a memory—not a single memory, to be sure, but an entire event played out from the middle of October through the early winter. It was perhaps my greatest hunting season ever, not just in terms of game killed, but for the memories it yielded. I'll recount some of the events here, not just for you, but for me also, so that they may become more clearly etched in my file of unforgettable events.

After spring gobbler hunting on May 1, 1991, I pulled back into the driveway to see a sickening sight: our new home had been virtually destroyed by fire. It was a devastating loss, and after the initial shock had worn off, every minute of every day was spent rebuilding. By late summer the house was nearly finished. On September 27, just three months from the start of rebuilding, my wife and I moved back in. I was exhausted and literally spent the next several days in bed. By the time squirrel season began a few weeks later, I desperately needed some woods time to wind down and recuperate.

The first day of squirrel season was a misty, rainy day, but it felt like heaven to be in the woods again. I spent almost the entire day there, drinking in the silence and absorbing the feeling of the changing colors. I limited out on squirrels and saw countless others that I would hunt and kill in the next two weeks. The feeling of relaxation and the calm of being back out hunting were indescribable. It was exactly what I needed.

The Pennsylvania rabbit season began on November 2, but I decided to hunt fall turkeys for a few days before breaking out the dogs and my rabbit gear. I had a few good chances to kill a turkey each time out, but other hunters and circumstances always kept the birds out of gun range. By Wednesday, the fourth day, I gave up and took the dogs out for their first day of hunting. It was a great afternoon, and after several good runs, three cottontails were laying on the tailgate of the truck as I put the dogs away. Later, while I was cleaning the bunnies, the phone rang. It was my cousin, Bud, with whom I had been hunting turkeys.

"Hey, I roosted about a dozen birds this evening. You want to go in the morning?"

"Yeah, I'll give it a try," I replied. "I'll dig out the camo and meet you at five o'clock."

With the help of Bud's late-afternoon scouting, he and I both took fall turkeys the next morning, and I was well on my way to having a banner hunting season. Before the rabbit season began, I was so anxious to hunt that I had made the statement to Bill and my other friends that I was going to kill 60 rabbits this season. In our part of Pennsylvania where rabbits are not real plentiful, this would be quite a feat. In my best season eight years earlier, I had taken 56 rabbits, something I thought I could never duplicate.

Of course, I should say here numbers don't always reflect a successful hunt, and I've been on great hunts that yielded very few rabbits. But lacking any other reasonable means to keep track of "how well we did," it makes sense to count the rabbits killed, and most rabbit hunters I know can tell you fairly accurately "how they did" during the season. As I've said before, no rabbits we kill are wasted.

After taking the Fall turkey, my rabbit season progressed with little fanfare. The weather was warm and dry, and it took the dogs a few hunts to settle down into serious rabbit hunting. Most of the time I was hunting alone and really enjoying it—just me and a pack of four or five hounds, the way it's supposed to be. Other times, Bud, Bill, or someone else would join me for a day or two.

Some hunts are etched into my mind so vividly it's almost like they happened yesterday. Here I am posed with a beautiful Pennsylvania gobbler taken in 1992. I have been blessed with many "special seasons."

The first really memorable rabbit hunt came when Bill was off work unexpectedly one day. It had rained, certainly not a deluge, but enough to wet the ground. Bill and I hit the woods about 9:00 and were anxious to get in a few hours before it heated up again. It was already 50°F and warming up fast.

We were in a spot we had never hunted before. It had great looking cover, but for the first 20 minutes or so everything was pretty quiet. Suddenly Bill yelled the cherished word . . . "Rabbit!"

The dogs hesitatingly picked up the scent and slowly lined up for the chase. Soon they were moving up the hill to my left, picking up speed with every bark.

The six-dog pack belonged to me and contained my three experienced dogs, Ralphie, Lightning, and Annie Oakley; one semi-trained two-year-old, Meg; a yearling tricolor, Jet; and a new pup, Sherri-Red. I had no idea how all the youngsters would run with the older dogs, but as most know, pups have to be trained and gain experience some way. Things started out well, and the pack, tightly bunched, was now about 200 yards out and turning downhill.

On this day, the dogs were running like those times we all dream about. The rabbit had gotten by me and was heading back to the jump site where Bill was waiting. The dogs were stretched out like a long red, white, and black snake as they threaded their way through the thicket. We hadn't seen the cottontail yet, but knew it was only a matter of time. You pray for days like this when the dogs really "lock on". . . and they were locked on!

The beagle train looped Bill once again and was coming my way. I saw the rabbit loping toward me, but much farther to the left than I had expected. The 1100 followed him for a few bounds, and then went off . . . he folded instantly. The hounds got almost to the fallen bunny, but then veered sharply right and headed downhill.

"Another rabbit!" I half yelled, half whispered back toward Bill.
Bill replied something like, "I know that!"

Still leaning against the maple tree where I had shot the first bunny, I saw the other cottontail step out on a game trail 60 yards in front of me. He was casually preening and listening to the dogs. He sat there for a minute or two, then hopped forward as Ralphie's coarse bark turned his way. The dogs crossed the trail, and then slithered up the hill again.

"Man, what a nice run!" I thought.

The dogs swung around again and started toward Bill for the second time. I half expected his gun to go off, but then I caught movement to my left. There he was, sneaking back uphill again! Two quick snap shots from the 1100 sent him tumbling. Bill and six wagging tails soon joined in my jubilation. Wish you could have been there!

While I was cleaning the two rabbits, Ralphie got up another and the dogs locked on in similar fashion and tore off over the same ground. I hurried my field-dressing operation and jockeyed around for a better spot where the rabbit had already made two passes.

I saw him coming, but he was on down the ridge and heading for Bill. One crisp "Bang!" from Bill's Winchester was the cymbal highlighting this great beagle orchestra. One more bunny would fall that morning and two more would be pushed to holes, an excellent day in a hot and dry early season.

Bill, although carrying only one rabbit, said it best when describing the morning.

"I've always said you don't have to have a whole lot of rabbits to have a good time. The way those dogs ran this morning, it just doesn't get any better than this!"

The memory of that great hunt was filed away to be talked about more than once in the months ahead.

Although the author hunted much of the 1991 season alone, once in awhile a friend would join him for an afternoon hunt. Here John Carson rests with Ralphie and Lightning after a good outing.

The early rabbit season continued. Very little out of the ordinary happened, which is the way I like it sometimes. I lost no dogs, I felt pretty good, hunted almost every day, and checked out a few new hunting spots. The early season would soon be over, and I thought little about the idea of shooting 60 rabbits for the season, as that seemed out of reach now. In New York and other states where I've hunted that mark would be nothing special, but here in southwestern Pennsylvania it would be an exceptional year.

One afternoon while hunting a familiar thicket close to home, the dogs really locked onto a bunny and I killed him after an exceptional chase. (I relate this entire run in Ch. 5, "Memories of Our Greatest Chases," and called it, 'The Crab Apple Flat Run'.) I was impressed with the dogs' performance and wondered why they can be so good on certain days. At this point I realized that if I was going to kill 60 rabbits, most of it was going to depend on the dogs' performance during the late season. I finished the early season with 25 rabbits. Not bad, but I had done better in other years, and I was still a long way from 60.

In Pennsylvania, you can hunt nothing else while the deer season is underway, so I concentrated on putting some venison in the freezer. With some bad luck and poor shooting, I failed to kill a nice buck that surprised me on opening morning. Bud and I got together again and hunted the next couple of days. On Thursday, another hunter jumped two bucks that both came sprinting my way. One accidentally ran into my .30-06 bullet, and I had a nice six-pointer. On Monday of the next week, I made a very good, one-shot kill on a doe that slipped out of the woods I had been watching. I marveled at how well things were going and was anxious to get back to rabbit hunting after Christmas.

The late season, like the early one, got off to a slow and uneventful start. I hunted with Bill the first day and we jumped few rabbits. The week went on about the same way: I continued to kill a few bunnies each day, but worked hard for them. The dogs, although running better than they had during the dry fall, had good days and bad days.

But then good things started happening. One morning, while hunting a small spot I hadn't been to yet that year, I made a couple of good shots and quickly collected two nice cottontails. The dogs soon opened on another and I missed it as it slipped under a cattle fence. As the dogs approached the fence, another rabbit shot down through the pasture and the dogs continued the chase. They ran those bunnies for the next hour or so, with both rabbits staying tight together the whole time. It's rare, but it happens. I finally killed one of those rabbits, and another a short time later. It was a smooth, exciting hunt and the dogs were tucked away in the truck by 1:00 P.M. as heavy rain began falling. It was one of the rare days when I took a limit of four rabbits.

New Year's Day brought a new hunting partner, Tim Abraham, my friend Jim's son. Jim had hosted and appeared on both of my rabbit hunting videos and had asked me to take Timmy hunting. Timmy had never killed a rabbit.

It turned out to be another good hunt. Tim jumped the first rabbit and the dogs ran it back in record time. I had Tim positioned correctly, but the rabbit spotted him and sprinted away, only to run into my load of No. 7s. The dogs quickly found another, and this time the bunny came hopping right for Tim. We could not have planned it any better, and Tim was elated to have taken his first bunny ever!

Later that day, the dogs had another good, long run, and after jockeying around quite a bit, I was able to get Tim in the right spot again. His second rabbit! The dogs brought us another an hour later, and I left the woods with my 40th bunny of the season, plus a very happy teenager. Tim had seen some good dog work and was beginning to understand how I felt about rabbit hunting. It was a day he would remember for a long time.

With three weeks to go, I felt that a 60-rabbit season was surely possible, but I know how things can go, and I know how Pennsylvania can be in January. (The Pennsylvania rabbit season actually extends into the New Year for a few weeks, as it does in many other states.)

Another of the more memorable events of the season happened on January 8. Bud and I met at a spot we had been to only once during the early, hot and dry season. Now it was a frosty morning and the dogs had a tough time finding any bunnies at first, but finally got one going off an old abandoned railroad bed. Bud and I both saw the bunny sneaking back a couple times, but couldn't get a shot at him. Finally the dogs settled into a thicket above us, and began running the perimeter.

"That's a different bunny," I called out to Bud.

"Oh, come on! How do you know that?" he replied.

"I'm telling you, that rabbit crossed this railroad bed three times, now all of a sudden he's running that thicket? No way. That's a different bunny."

We moved in on the thicket, and when the dogs reached the other side I moved in even closer. Bud was still skeptical, but understood the rabbit was clearly running the boundaries of this thicket. Bud closed in on my far left.

I was now kneeling down and looking up under the heavy canopy of crabapple trees, almost like looking into a wide tunnel. The thicket was fairly clear underneath, at least clear enough that I could shoot if I saw the bunny.

"We've got him now!" I thought. "He's been through here at least three times and we're in good gun range now."

Seconds later a rabbit came barreling from left to right, zigzagging through the maze of crabapples trees. I followed him the best I could, and touched the trigger when he sprinted through an opening about 30 yards out. He tumbled, but I was unsure how hard he was hit. I took three steps toward him to make sure he was going to stay put, when suddenly a second rabbit came tearing through going in the opposite direction! I spun around on one foot and fired a foot or so over the disappearing cottontail.

I got to the first rabbit about the time Ralphie broke out of the heavy brush to see what all the shooting was about. I showed him the fallen bunny, then put him on the trail of the second. Ralph picked up the trail, made a few barks, and was about to disappear into the brush when he slammed on the brakes. The other bunny was right there, just a few feet from where I had shot at him! I had hit two rabbits within seconds of each other, each going in different directions!

Bud came crashing over. "What's all the racket over here?"

"I told you that was a different rabbit," I said. "One of these is from the railroad bed, the other was in here. I got both of them at practically the same time!"

Bud never said a word. It was another moment for the "file," and my 49th and 50th rabbits.

With almost two weeks to go in the season, I felt uneasily confident about shooting another ten rabbits. I called Brian Salley and we planned a hunt together. Brian had seen my rabbit videos and had come to my home early in the summer to buy two pups from me. It would be our first hunt together.

Heavy falling snow made for a tough hunt that day. The dogs ran well, however, and in the pouring white stuff I managed to shoot three rabbits while Brian took one. We jumped at least 14 rabbits in the Indiana County swamp, but it was snowing so hard that we could barely see 15 yards in front of us. We finally had to quit, but vowed to return on another day.

Very bad weather moved in, with six more inches of powdery snow blasting everything white. I hunted a couple days in five-degree weather, but managed to kill only one more bunny. All the rabbits were forced to ground, and I was forced inside.

On January 18, I hunted alone in a small thicket behind my grandmother's. Snow still covered everything and it was a balmy 25°F. At one point, without any warning, the dogs suddenly chased three cottontails out of a small patch of vines, all at the same time, and I totally missed each one of them! I stood there with my mouth hanging open, as the dogs followed the trails to a cluster of holes about 100 yards uphill.

I was upset with myself. Rabbits were getting extremely hard to come by in the harsh weather and I had blown a very good chance. I kicked myself. I should have certainly gotten at least one of them.

The dogs and I kicked up several more rabbits, but each one holed quickly before any could get back around to me. I swung the dogs around and headed for the truck. We were walking along, with nothing really happening, when Lightning started to whimper. I could tell she had found a hot bunny track. The bunny must have heard us coming and slipped away. She stuck with the track, and then Ralphie and Annie also got interested. They took the rabbit up along the right side of the thicket and the chase heated up out across the top of the woods.

For some reason, the rabbit passed by many holes, and by the sound of the chase it appeared he was bending back along the far-left side of the brush, and maybe my way. I spun around to watch the small wooded section where Lightning had first started barking. There he was! The big woods bunny came bounding through the woods so quickly that I barely had time to throw the gun on him. As I pulled the trigger, I can remember telling myself he was out of range. The rabbit went down anyway, with at least one pellet breaking his neck.

The dogs were still a ways off when I hoisted the bunny up and took a good look at him. He was a beauty: a fully mature woods cottontail, perhaps three, four years old. He was also my 56th of the season and so pretty that I carried him back to the truck carefully and saved him to be mounted. I stood there scratching my head. How could I have missed three cottontails streaking dead away in open brush, then make a spectacular shot on one an hour later? I had no answer. I guess that's just rabbit hunting, and I can remember some of my misses in great detail . . . even when I'm trying to forget them.

At 4:00 A.M. on January 20, it started snowing again. four inches of new powder, piled on top of several inches of old snow, blasted every conceivable piece of rabbit cover. They went to ground again. This was the last week of the season. I hunted the next two days anyway, but didn't come up with any bunnies.

With only four days of Pennsylvania rabbit hunting left, I left home at 7:00 A.M. and arrived at Brian's at 9:00 A.M. The weather was warming slightly and we had decided to hit The Swamp again. The morning began perfectly, with the dogs running very well in the melting snow. By noon, I had killed two rabbits and Brian had taken another. Then things really fell apart. Ralphie and Lightning were attacked by some unknown animal back in the laurels. Ralphie, with blood streaming from five puncture wounds, needed immediate medical attention. Brian and I spent the rest of the day at a vet's office in Indiana, Pennsylvania. (See Ch. 18, "The Mystery of Laurel Swamp.")

The good news from the vet was that Ralphie would fully recover. The bad news was that I lost Ralphie, my pack leader, for the rest of the season. More bad news: another storm was moving in.

On Thursday, the next morning, it was pouring sheets of rain when I got up. I could barely see across the yard to the dog pens, and the forecast said this would quickly change to snow. I knew most of the rabbits would be holed already, and in most cases any jumped would go to ground right away. But I had to try. Another bad snowstorm would virtually wipe out the two remaining days of the season. Rabbit hunting in this weather seemed unthinkable. In other years, I would have simply called it quits, but I was now obsessed with having a 60-rabbit season. I know it sounds silly, and down the road in years to come it may seem an insignificant thing, but at the time it seemed very important. Ten years later it still does.

I parked at a friend's house near good rabbit cover, put on my raingear, and dropped the dogs out onto the soggy ground. It was 9:50 A.M.

Taking Ralphie out hunting was out of the question, so I had my three most experienced "girls" with me: Lightning, Annie Oakley, and O-Mega. I entered the cover cautiously, looking intently for sitting rabbits. The dogs worked under everything that remotely looked like it could hide a bunny. Although I hadn't hunted here for nearly four years, I was familiar with the area, as my friend, Joe Mikluscak, and his family own the property. I had hunted it many times in years gone by.

I checked all the usual spots where we normally jumped rabbits, but found nothing. The rain never let up, but wasn't as bad as I had anticipated. As long as you didn't face into the wind, it was at least tolerable. The dogs were hunting well, but I knew they would tire easily and get disgusted in this weather if we didn't find any rabbits soon.

A little more than an hour into the hunt, the dogs entered a very thick section of crabapples and rip-shins on the outskirts of a thicket we call "The Pines." Lightning started a rabbit, and the two other dogs cut in immediately. They moved the rabbit straight out quickly, then turned slowly left and downhill. I didn't know how they would run without Ralphie, but things seemed to be going well. I was expecting the rabbit to hole at his first opportunity, however.

It was difficult to keep track of the dogs in the pouring rain, but they seemed to be somewhere out to the left and slowly coming around the hillside. I was in about the best place I could be, an open section of woods just 35 yards or so from where the dogs found the bunny. I had only one advantage: The bunny had absolutely no idea I was with the dogs when they kicked him up.

The chase was coming my way. I shook some water from my soaked gloves and tightened my grip on the forearm. The dogs were still over the rise when all of a sudden, there he was! He was coming straight for me at full throttle, and I remember thinking, "Why is he coming so hard?"

I'm an instinctive shooter, and rarely aim the shotgun, so before I could even think about it the 1100 slid up my wet coat, and then a sharp "BANG" cut through the icy rainstorm. The cottontail, hit in the head, tumbled end over end and crashed to a stop ten feet in front of me. Number 59!

The dogs arrived on the scene wet but happy, and after much deserved praise went back to hunting. It was 11 o'clock.

"Do you think we could scrounge up one more before this turns into one heck of a snowstorm?" I asked them as we continued working the heavy rip-shins into the main pine thicket. No answer.

It wasn't going to be easy. I checked out every clump of brush, every stump, logs, rock piles, anything that could hide another ball of fur. The dogs did the same. Another hour went by. The water on my hands and legs had started to freeze by the time I reached the far side of the pine thicket.

I saw the dogs' tails 75 yards out into another small thicket that came right up to the edge of a cornfield. The dogs didn't make a peep, but suddenly a cotton-tail came out of the field, sprinted across my left flank, and slipped into the pines. He was hopelessly out of range, but I let fly a desperation shot. The dogs, alerted by the shot, smelled around and picked up the trail. A few seconds later, they disappeared back into the pine grove.

I was in another good spot. A swirl a brush lead out to the edge of the thicket and ended right in front of me, making a natural runway for any cottontail coming this way. Another opening to my right offered me a good view of the field and the path the rabbit took to get out of the area. I was pretty sure he'd come back that way.

He did, but I was asleep at the switch and he got through the opening without my seeing him. When the three female beagles went through in full bay, I kicked myself for being so lax . . . or blind! How did I miss seeing him?

They pushed the bunny up through the edge of a strip mine and slowly back around to the edge of the cornfield. I was proud of the dogs . . . they were running very well. Ralphie's job as pack leader could be in serious jeopardy from one of the girls! I was surprised the rabbit hadn't holed up yet.

Finally, I saw the dogs coming down the extreme edge of the cornfield. Why couldn't I see the rabbit? He surely had run the entire edge of the field and had slipped around me. I cursed under my breath for this rotten break, but then all of the dogs screamed together—the unmistakable sound of a jump and sight chase.

They were all coming straight at me now, in some sort of confused mob scene. I saw the rabbit pull ahead of them and then break left, affording me an unbelievably easy shot. It was . . . and I missed him cleanly! I tried to regain my composure, took a second shot, and missed again! The cottontail veered sharply left, then sprinted for the bank of the strip mine. The 1100 went off again in a desperate attempt to keep him from reaching heavy cover, but he did anyway. I hit him, but didn't know how hard. Now he'll go to the first hole he comes to.

Disgusted with myself, I shook my head and jammed more shells in my water-soaked gun as I reached the last bank I saw him go over. And there he was, under some dewberry vines where he'd taken refuge. He saw me and took off, but I finally made a decent shot and he fell into another patch of vines a short distance away. The dogs filed past and Meg and Lightning played tug of war with him as they happily carried No. 60 to me!

The rain was coming down even harder now, yet I didn't even notice. I was too caught up in the moment of admiring the rabbit and praising the dogs. The bunny was soaked and tattered from the dogs pulling on it, but it might as well have been a ten-point buck to me. I drank in the moment until the cold, and now snow, forced me to move on.

I circled the edge of the strip mine, not hunting now, just heading the dogs back in the general direction of the truck. I admired the stamina they displayed all season and relished the loyalty they showed me. They are far from perfect hounds, but they have always given their very best.

A quarter-mile from the truck, another large cottontail suddenly flew out from in front of the dogs. I threw the gun up and rolled him as he was about to enter a large patch of broom sage along the strip. Soaked to the skin, I didn't want the dogs running off. The cottontail was an exceptionally large one, and perfectly dry. I marveled at how these animals can survive in almost any conditions. He was my 61st rabbit of the season and I knew I would shoot no more in Pennsylvania that year. I hustled the dogs back to the truck, avoiding as much rabbit cover as I could. It's funny. First I can't seem to buy a rabbit, and then I'm trying not to encounter any! At 1:30 P.M., I boosted the dogs back into the box on the truck, and my 1991 Pennsylvania hunting season came to a close.

In concluding this chapter, it is my sincere hope that no one feels that the recollection of shooting 61 rabbits in a season was a way of boasting or a display of my prowess as a rabbit hunter. It is not meant to be. In fact, with the time I had, and with the help of good dogs, which I had, another person could have done the same.

No, this chapter is simply a way of recalling all the great moments, the stories, and the events of a truly outstanding season, and a way of sharing them with others. As I said at the beginning of this book, beagling is not just the pursuit, not just the kill. It is the whole and complete experience of hound, cottontail, and hunter all combined into a medley only those who have heard and experienced it can truly understand.

The real hidden treasure in a hunting season such as this one is not how many rabbits fell before the dogs, but the thrilling, and yes, unforgettable moments it provided. I can see clearly the three cottontails flying out of the brush and streaking away unscathed by my poor shooting, Lightning carrying a bunny for 100 yards after a friend hit it and it got away, Timmy holding up his first cottontail ever. And I can recall vividly the scene in Laurel Swamp when I thought I had lost my friend and loyal companion Ralphie, maybe forever. The list goes on and on.

When all the rabbits are cleaned and eaten, when trusted dogs of years past fade away, and flesh and bones are so weary that they can no longer hold a shotgun, there is little left but the memories of past and great hunts. Oh, those memories . . .

Denny Malone strolls down the beach on Beaver Island Michigan with four hounds raring to go in the fall of 1994. It was one of the most exciting places we ever hunted and for the next ten fall seasons we hunted the wilds of the Upper Peninsula.

What makes the hare seem a much tougher quarry is that he lives in much smaller and more remote areas than the cottontail.

20

SNOWSHOE HARE HUNTING

I know this is a book on cottontail hunting, but what cottontail hunter hasn't dreamed of the chance to hunt a creature that holds almost a mythical place in the imagination. A large rabbit that turns as white as the driven snow and can live in weather and terrain harsh enough to hinder humans from going after him, is an interesting animal to be sure. I would be amiss if I didn't mention him and pass on a little of what I know about the snowshoe hare.

First off, I think I should dispel the theory of the snowshoe being such an elusive animal that he is almost impossible to bag. He isn't; and with a few good dogs and a little advanced planning he's almost as easy to bring home as his smaller cousin, the cottontail. I can tell you, however, that it is an enormous thrill to get one after hunting nothing but cottontails all of your hunting life. What makes the hare seem a much tougher quarry is the simple fact that he lives in a much smaller area (in the United States), and in more remote locations than the cottontail. The hare may live across all of Canada, but few of us have access to hunt him there. Also, since the hare lives in colder, denser swamps, far away from populated areas, his range is again limited to only certain states. The hunters living in states such as Michigan, New York, Maine, and Massachusetts, are fortunate indeed to have this type of game animal nearby.

Hares, although commonly called rabbits, are in the same family as the cottontail or the other rabbits, *Leporidae*, but belong to a separate order of creatures called *Lagomorpha*. The main difference between the hares and rabbits is that the hare is born with hair and ready to hop around in just a few hours, while the rabbit is born naked and requires many days of development before it can move around on its own. The snowshoe hare's scientific name is *Lepus americanus*. The cottontail is known in scientific circles as *Sylvilagus floridanus*.

My first encounter with a snowshoe hare was in West Virginia. My cousin and I had made at least two trips into the wilderness of the Back Bone Mountain

area, about 100 miles from our home, before I finally killed one. We were hunting national forest land, knew little about the area, and neither our dogs nor we
were very good in the heavy snow and rough terrain. But, somehow we killed
our first snowshoe hare there.

Later, I made several trips to upstate New York to hunt hares with Zef Selca.
The biggest advantage any hunter could have when wanting to pursue hares is
knowing someone who has hunted them before. After awhile, it's not hard to
spot good hare cover, but for out-of-state hunters, securing permission to hunt
and then not knowing the terrain are the two biggest stumbling blocks. I guess
it's like any hunting: You need a place to hunt, and you need someone to show
you the ropes. It's very possible to hunt state and federal ground on your own
for hares, but count on spending a couple days just feeling your way around.

The author with a couple beautiful white snowshoe hares taken along the Saint Lawrence Seaway
in upstate New York. Notice how the hares blend perfectly with the background.

For the past seven or eight years I have also ventured to the islands in upper Michigan to hunt snowshoe hares in October. This has yielded some thrilling hunts. I catalog a great deal of this Michigan hare hunting in my second book, *I'd Rather Be Rabbit Hunting.*

Hares are hunted in much the same way cottontails are. Dogs are just about a necessity, and longer-legged beagles can be a big advantage in deeper snow. Hares will be found in the denser parts of brushy ridges in the mountains, and in cedar and pine-infested swamps and lowlands. Hares like the very thickest cover they can find. In New York, where we hunted several times, hares readily ate cedar and barked red brush or any saplings available. Hare tracks are easily distinguishable from cottontails because of their size and the recognizable large hind prints. I have also seen hares cover nine to ten feet in a single bound, leaving unbelievably large tracks in the snow.

A hare hunt goes about much like any cottontail hunt. The dogs are released into likely looking cover; the hunters follow along working through the brush. Normally you don't see a snow-shoe bounding away, as they will slip off at the sound of the hunter's approach, and the first sign that one is up and running will be the dogs barking. Once the hare is off and running, it's the same as cot-tontail hunting, as the hunters will jockey around until a suitable opening to wait in is found.

Because the hare lives in such thick surroundings, openings can be hard to find, and much of the shooting will be very close. In most

Hares are hunted much the same way as cottontails, but as this picture shows they are tough to see in the dense jungle they live in. Once the snow comes, they are almost invisible.

situations I found my improved cylinder with No. 6s or 7s worked fine on hares, the same as it did on cottontails. If you're fortunate enough to run the hare where some openings, tractor paths, or cleared property lines exist, then you might want to use a No. 6 high base case, but in most cases your favorite cot-tontail load will easily bring down a hare if he's in range.

The hare will run a much larger circle than the cottontail depending on how much pressure the dogs put on him. The faster the dogs chase him, the farther the hare will go before he begins his turn. Good trailing dogs will eventually push the hare back to the vicinity where he was jumped, so don't worry if your dogs go out of hearing range for awhile.

It is said that hares never hole up but spend their entire lives on top of the ground. After hunting them for several winters, I believe this is only partially true. We have witnessed hares taking refuge in holes at the bases of fallen trees, and found very few out in territory loaded with tracks. Also, in very cold and harsh weather hares will either hole up or sit so still in their forms that it is virtually impossible to get them moving unless the dog actually blunders into one. This makes for some very poor hunting. The best hare hunting seems to be earlier in the season, before the truly sub-zero weather moves in. From accounts from veteran snowshoe hunters, the true banner days are early in March as hares start to move about to breed. Of course, those living in actual hare hunting states are privileged and better apt to hitting these good hunting days in March.

Hares are good to eat, but those living in cedar will have to be soaked and rinsed several times before cooking. My friend, Bill, likes to boil them, then deep fry the pieces rolled in batter. It's good, but not quite as good as cottontail.

After you've hunted cottontails for most of your life, it's only natural any hunter might want to try something different. Hunting hares is certainly a new and different experience, and I think every cottontail hunter should give it a try once in his lifetime.

A snowshoe hare with his white winter coat.

Tony Rinaldi (left) and Bob Clarke (right) examine a large hare taken in upper Michigan in 1998. Notice only the feet have turned white at this time, but what giant feet they are!!

This is Old Clyde Burnsworth (the dog dealer) and a few of his hounds.

21

THE GIFT

The pickup jolted to a stop and before the creaks and cracks could even die away Jack heard the sound of muffled barking coming from the dog pens behind the barn. It was still warm for September and the dust swirled around the truck, catching Jack's attention. He looked at the rough, old buildings and the small broken-down training pen on the hillside nearby.

"What on earth am I doing here?" he said quietly to himself. He reached for the key to turn the truck on again, but stopped short at the sound of a raspy, strained voice.

"Well, don't jest set in the truck, man, git out and stretch your legs. I tol' ya it was kite a drive out 'ere!"

"Yeah, it sure was. Pretty though. How do you and your brothers ever spend so much time in town?" Jack asked, not knowing what else to say.

"Ehhhhhh, we take turns drivin'. . .ya know we all like a little nip . . . an' ain't much around here. Ya have to 'cuse my voice," old Burnsworth said. "I gut a touch of sore throat yelling at the dogs and such."

Jack looked over the elderly man as he led the way past the dilapidated barn through piles of neglected manure and into the sunshine behind the huge structure. Clyde Burnsworth was somewhere near 70; tall, lean, and weathered like an old piece of rawhide. He was a likeable sort, and although Jack had seen him in town many times, and exchanged pleasantries with him on occasion, he still knew little about him or his family, which lived scattered on nearby hills. The fleeting thought of what he was doing here occurred again, but was broken quickly by the old man's grating voice and the barking of the dogs.

"Yeah, I know, I got quite a collection of 'em. Thes'ons over here is justa bunch of cold trailers I keep for those guys that always want those mouthy dogs. I don't have much use for them. I got some better'ons 'ere that have all the papers . . . run a pretty good rabbit. I got some general purpose hounds there, and I got a few I just hunt with, plus I got some pups." The old man droned on as Jack tried to focus on a few individual dogs, and the myriad of pups clamoring for attention and jumping at the wire.

The rhetoric continued for some time as Jack tried to keep up. This dog has this sire, these are doubled registered, and these are not. Grade dogs over here.

"I say, Man, ya paying attention? I said these ain't for sale. Well unless the offer's one I cain't refuse!" The old man snickered.

Jack turned slowly around as if in an old-time movie. Dogs everywhere, how do you choose? After a long time Jack noticed a dog sort of by herself, and with her were four half-grown pups that looked very much like the very dark, almost blue blanket of what he took to be the mother.

"What are those dogs there?" Jack inquired.

"Ahhhh, ya don't want nothin' like that, Son! Well, that's just my regular huntin' bitch. Not a bad rabbit runner, but she got frisky one night and got caught with one of these other dogs when I was feedin'. Heck, man, I don't even know who's the daddy, if ya know what I mean?" old Burnsworth laughed a long raspy exchange.

An hour later, after Jack had listened and looked over the entire herd, he still hadn't seen anything that had caught his eye. Now they were back at the barn entrance where the huntin' dog and her older pups were. Jack tried not to let Clyde know he was studying the group again. Each pup was distinctive in her own right, but Jack couldn't help notice how similar they all were and how they looked so much like the mother.

"Heck's, man, ya don't want one of those. Ahhhhhhh, I can see that's what you're goin' ta git. Man, I had visions of makin' a couple hundred bucks today. Heck, man, which one ya want?"

Old Clyde sounded pretty disgusted, but still not too unhappy to get rid of one of the "mistakes."

"Well, what do ya want for them?" Jack asked.

"Shoot, man, I don't know. Never thought 'bout it. Ya know I've fed 'em for three months and I gave 'em one shot. How's $75?"

"Sounds fair enough. Just grab whichever one ya'd like to get out of there, they all seem the same to me."

Burnsworth acted like he didn't even hear Jack, just opened the door and grabbed the first pup that came running. "Don't know why ya want a dawg like this when I got some real rabbit machines over there. Could have made a couple hundred dollars . . ."

Jack knew he had overstayed his welcome and scooped up the pup from the old farmer's arms, slipping him the $75 at the same time. "Well, thanks, I appreciate it.

I'll buy ya a drink next time you're in town . . ."

Jack stumbled back through the cluttered barn as he could hear Clyde still grumbling in the background.

"Don't know why ya want a dawg like that. Hey, ya know I don't have no papers for that thing . . ."

Jack closed the pickup and quickly turned the key. He hoped he could smooth things over the next time he saw Burnsworth in town.

Once on the highway, Jack could get a better look at his $75 purchase. The pup's initial exuberance had settled down to mild curiosity as she peered out the windshield and licked Jack now and then.

The pup was beautiful. A perfectly ringed white tail gave way to four almost perfect white socks, and blended into a white chest, framed very lightly by a thin line of tan that blended into the jet black-bluish blanket of the main coat. Jack could not have picked a prettier puppy if he would have taken hours to choose. He hoped Jerry would be pleased.

On the way home Jack thought a lot about Jerry. Tears came to his eyes as he thought about him still lying in the hospital. Doctors said if everything went well, he would be home for Christmas. Jack hoped so with all his heart. Jack hoped he and the pup would be ready.

The puppy got the royal treatment for the next few days, and Jack made Sherri swear not to tell Jerry about her. A name for her came to Jack automatically on the way home. No thinking about it; she would be called "Promise."

Promise was a quick student and within no time Jerry had her barking at wild bunnies that wandered into the backyard in the evening. She still had a lot to learn, but she was coming along. Her fast chop grew more excited the closer she got to a bunny, and Sherri and Jack enjoyed many evenings just listening to her. The runs were short, but grew in length each time out, and Jack knew she would be ready when Jerry came home. To keep the secret, Jack had also made a backup pen at his brother's place. The plan was to take Promise to Sam's a few days before Jerry came home. Everything would be ready soon.

Jack got a few days of hunting in during November, but refused to kill any rabbits over Promise. "That's going to be Jerry's job," he'd say, "shooting the first rabbit over his dog."

Promise was now a beauty. A full-grown hound with sleek sides and thick, muscular legs, she seemed as if she could run for hours without tiring. Jack kept taking her out, and Sam trailed along now and then.

"That's a fine hound," Sam would compliment his brother. "I'll bet you paid big money for that dog."

Jack would just smile and agree. "Yeah. That's a fine hound, no doubt about it."

Jack spent every moment away from work (or when he wasn't running Promise) at the hospital. Jerry was learning to walk again, and Jack gave his son all the help he could. Finally, a couple weeks before Christmas, the doctors met with Jack and Sherri.

"We've done all we can for him here," they said. "He's a lucky boy. He'll be all right, but it will take some time. He'll probably do better at home now."

Jack and Sherri were ecstatic, and the next few days were nothing but a pleasant blur as they got Jerry settled in at home. He hobbled around, and went to therapy almost daily. He even talked about hunting again. Promise was secretly hidden at Uncle Sam's and all her toys, bowls, and stuff were hidden behind the garage at her new kennel. Sherri and Jack made sure Jerry didn't even look in that direction.

One Saturday, just a week before Christmas, Jack and Jerry were riding through town when Jack suddenly pulled the pickup over.

"I got to run in here for a second," Jack said to his son, motioning toward the bar across the street.

"But Dad, you said you quit drinkin'," Jerry moaned.

"It's okay, Jerry, I'll be right back." Jack gave him a reassuring smile and Jerry knew it was okay somehow. Jerry was in no condition to follow him anyway, so he just sat there dumbfounded.

Jack rubbed his hand down the side of an old truck he passed on the way to the bar. "Yep, that's his truck for sure," he said silently.

Jack strolled into the bar as he had done many times before. Several guys gave him a friendly greeting, and he quickly caught sight of old Burnsworth and his two brothers.

"Clyde, how are you? Jess? George? I'll buy you that drink now if you'll let me? The dog has turned out to be a fine, young hound." Jack gave the bartender the familiar glance and motioned for drinks for all three men.

"Yeah, well I guess that will be alright. Still don't know why ya wanted a hound like that. The others are running right well too. Must have been a good daddy in 'ere somewhere!" The old man laughed.

The men got their drinks, Jack paid the few dollars it cost, made a little conversation, then started toward the door.

"Where ya goin, Man? Ain't ya goin ta have a drink with us before ya run off, Man?"

"Naaaa, can't, my boy's waiting for me. I quit drinking anyway. You guys take care going home—see ya." With that, Jack stepped through the door and walked across the street. Jerry was pleased to see him come back so soon, but it was such a mysterious incident, he felt strange about asking his dad any further questions.

They said little more about it on the way home.

"Can we stop at Uncle Sam's on the way home Dad? I've only seen him once since I've been home."

"Now you know Sam is probably working today. I think he's coming over in a few days anyway, he has something he wants to show you. We'll see him soon enough."

Jerry was disappointed. Things were going slower than he had hoped. He wondered how soon before he might even be allowed back in the woods again. Dad was being very evasive, but Jerry was enjoying the time they were spending together. In his whole life he had never seen his dad so much. It was something he could get to like.

The next morning Jerry gingerly stepped out of the van from his therapy session and Jack motioned for him to follow him around the garage. Jack had meticulously cleaned all traces of Promise and had shined and washed the bowls. The pen looked brand new again.

"What's this?" Jerry asked with a puzzled look, "Are we getting a dog, Dad?"

"Well, it's a possibility. I thought since you are doing so well we might want to consider it," Jack shot back with a grin so big that it almost gave away the secret.

"Gee, Dad, that would be great!" Jerry said humbly. "But I am not sure when I might be able to train it. I can't walk 40 yards without taking a break."

"Ohhhh, you're doing fine. We'll just see what happens."

The plan was all set. Just one day before Christmas Sam was to bring Promise over to meet Jerry. They waited until late in the evening when Jerry had settled down in the living room, stretched out on the sofa.

"I heard a car pull up, Dad. Who would be coming over here this late?"

"Ah, that's Uncle Sam. He wanted to see ya before Christmas, and he worked late today. I'll go let him in."

"No, you take her in, Jack," Sam whispered. "I don't want him to think she's from me. I'll watch from the door."

Jack nodded his approval and gently took hold of the leash, where the little princess seemed to be enjoying all the special attention. Sam slipped in where he could see Jerry, and Jack led the beautiful hound straight into the living room.

"I'd like you to meet Promise. Jerr, it has been tough trying to hide her from you. She's all yours and it's time to bring her home."

Jerry was speechless, and everyone just looked at each other for a few seconds. Then Promise promptly put her feet up on the couch, as beagles do, and began to lick Jerry.

Sherri turned away to keep from crying and looked at Sam, who wasn't in much better shape. They walked into the kitchen and began pouring coffee, leaving father and son with the dog.

Jerry still couldn't say anything, so Jack began.

"I got her from old man Burnsworth, that's why I went into the bar last week, to sort of thank him. She's not perfect—got a lot to learn—but she can already circle a rabbit by herself . . ."

Jerry, still unsure if he could talk, choked back a few more tears and tried to speak. "That sure is a strange name, Promise. But Dad, you're wrong, she is perfect."

After a long silence Jack looked up to see Sam and Sherri back at the doorway again, drinking coffee silently, watching.

"Well, Jerry, the doctors say you're well enough to go on short hunts. We'll go over behind Uncle Sam's where we hunted lots of times. There are lots of tractor cuts in there and you won't have to be far from the truck. We'll go next week if I have a day off. You want to put Promise out in the kennel for the night?"

Promise in the kennel? The laughter grew louder as Promise jumped right up on the couch and everyone knew this dog wasn't headed for any kennel for the night. A couple hours later, after Sam had gone home, Jack and Sherri were finally in bed.

"Ya know, Jack, that was really something you did for Jerry. I've never seen you and him closer, but you're trying a little too hard. He still loves you y'know," Sherri said quietly.

Jack said nothing. In his mind he was already planning the rabbit hunt with Jerry and Promise. He was praying that things would go well.

With Christmas over, Jack had persuaded Jerry to let Promise sleep in the fancy dog box he had built, and she had actually spent the last two nights there. Jack had hunted all his life, had taken big game in many parts of the world, but he was never more nervous about anything than the hunt with Promise tomorrow. He had even secretly taken Promise to the spot just to see exactly where the rabbit might make his appearance.

You would have thought it was the first day of buck season, as the two men prepared for the hunt. It was a cool, perfect morning for hunting, but was going to warm up quickly. Jack knew that Jerry would be worn out way before noon, so it didn't matter. Promise *had* to ride up front on the way to the hunt, and Jack was so happy that the butterflies were finally subsiding; he didn't even care.

Once the truck pulled to a creaky stop in the field behind Sam's, all the preparation came to an end.

"Just let her go Jerr, she's been here before and knows what to do. You get your stuff and walk up the tractor path."

Promise worked the cover where she had jumped rabbits before, but it took a long time before she cut into a fresh track. Both men smiled as the cottontail jumped the path and entered a small sweet-corn field on the left. The path widened there and Jack, barking instructions, told Jerry to move up there.

Promise might not be perfect, but this was a perfect run. Her fast chop was easy to follow and she took the bunny to the far side of the corn and then turned around. With little warning the cottontail jumped onto the path and made a beeline for the thick bottom on the right. Jerry shouldered the gun quickly but his first shot went over. He pumped the gun like a professional and followed the rabbit again. Just before it was to leap into the thick brush, the gun roared again and the cottontail rolled into the shorter grass at the edge.

"Yes!!" came the shout from behind. "The first rabbit ever killed over Promise! Hold on, I'll get him for ya!"

The celebration between the two took longer than expected, and when the dog suddenly went quiet the two looked up to see Promise proudly carrying the prize down the trail.

"And she retrieves, Dad!"

Jack was elated. It was the first of several rabbits that Promise would bring around that day. It was an unforgettable hunt between father and son.

"Well, old man," Jack joked, "if you can hobble over to the little stream there we'll clean this rabbit up!"

Jack, carrying the rabbit, suddenly stopped and turned around to face Jerry again.

"Ya know, Jerr, there's something I been meanin' to tell ya. I, uh, I umm, I just—wanted to let you know—that I promise never to drink again. And I'm sorry, ya know, for the wreck and all . . . I didn't mean . . ."

"Yeah, I know Dad, I understand. I understand the name now, too. I hope you won't mention it anymore," he gave his dad a big smile.

Jack stood there relieved as if a ton of bricks had just been lifted from his shoulders. Jerry brushed past him limping toward the creek.

"Come on, old man," Jerry quipped. "Promise is barking again. And hey, Dad, Merry Christmas to you, too."

This is the scene of the son and dad together celebrating Jerry's first rabbit. Promise is seen carrying the rabbit back.

22

RABBIT HUNTING'S FUTURE

Anyone who has hunted rabbits for more than a few years will certainly tell you that things aren't what they once were. This is true with any kind of hunting, and rabbit hunting is no exception. In some cases, like deer and turkey, the hunting is actually better, as these species have learned to adapt and to live in proximity to humans.

If someone has come up with a clear, definitive answer as to why the rabbit population has been in a general decline over the past couple of decades, I'd surely like to meet him. In the fall, as hunters look forward to the coming seasons, newspapers and other outdoor publications are crammed with articles describing "the great rabbit disappearance," and each author has his or her opinion on which calamity has done the rabbit in for this year. Hunters in some areas report almost no shortage of bunnies, but most report a general scarcity.

No one particular cause can be cited for the rabbits' decline; it is probably a combination of things. One of the things that seems to have made the rabbit a tougher animal to hunt and find is his adaptability. In the 1950s and 1960s, rabbits were easily rousted in open fields and sparse brush. So what happened? Rabbits with a tendency to "field sit" were slowly killed off, and slightly smarter rabbits took their place. The rabbits simply adapted to survive, moving deeper into the brush and briars. There were probably just as many rabbits around, but by the 1970s they were just a wee bit tougher to find, and guys who had no dogs eventually gave up chasing them. This adaptation continues to this day, making the rabbit almost a total brush creature, and a more challenging game animal. Of course, some rabbits went the other way, moving in as close as they possibly could to homes and suburban developments.

These rabbits quickly learned that for the most part they are safe and generally left alone. The rabbit population does swing up and down from year to year, and it is thought that cottontail populations are on a seven-year cycle. I do believe in some years there are just as many rabbits as there ever were; it's just that they don't sit around where they can be killed easily. They've learned to adapt.

Another aspect in the rabbits' decline is tied directly to habitat. There are so many variables to this that I couldn't begin to list them all. Generally, however, the rabbit population follows the good brushy habitat. A perfect example is a section of woods directly across the road from my home. Thirty years ago, when I first moved in, it was an excellent spot for bunnies. The rabbits slowly thinned out in the next five years, and then a logger was given permission to cut down some of the trees. With an abundance of downed treetops, more open areas, and emergent growth, the rabbit population consequently blossomed, and I enjoyed great hunting for the next dozen years or so. This spot became my all-time favorite place to hunt.

Slowly the treetops rotted away and the live trees again began to shade the understory. Eventually the 50 acres reverted to an almost mature forest, with little brush below the trees. The rabbits dwindled and have been replaced by deer and turkeys. This isn't bad, but I miss my rabbit patch.

Although the future of rabbit hunting is cloudy, it will be with us for awhile yet. The rabbit has learned to adapt so well there will always be a huntable population. Here, Jeff Mitchell displays a trio of mountain cottontails taken in Fayette County, Pennsylvania, during the late winter season.

This scenario is happening all over the country. Many brushy areas and over-grown, abandoned farms are slowly becoming open woodlots, spelling doom for any serious rabbit hunting. This problem is especially acute here in Pennsylvania. There is good news here, however. Trees are valuable, everyone knows that, and it does not take long for landowners and loggers to strike up deals to harvest the trees. These cut woodlots are magnets for cottontails, but they can be frustrating to hunt. It usually takes a few years before some of the treetops and brush begin to rot down to allow good hunting.

One serious problem facing rabbit hunters is the fact that game and fish departments, forestry associations, and other conservation organizations are buy-ing up a lot of these reverting forestlands. Again this is not bad news, as the land will always be there, protected from unscrupulous developers, but in most cases the land is never developed for small game hunters. Deer licenses and turkey permits raise a ton of money for the various state game agencies; and the rabbit hunter is always second behind the wishes of an army of orange-clad deer hunters.

Open brush and mature timber are the deer hunters' mainstay, and so that's what game agencies manage for. Rabbit and small game hunters need to voice their opinion, and stress the fact that they buy licenses too. What's wrong with some of the land being managed for rabbit hunting? Deer and other game ani-mals will also use it. There are very few areas managed or set aside just for small game hunting. It is my humble opinion that most game agencies don't realize how important good brushy cover is for deer and certainly rabbit hunting.

Almost all the raptorial birds have been placed on the federal protected species list, creating another obstacle to any serious rabbit population boom. Hawks and owls routinely raid my training pen, and it is not hard to find traces of rabbit kills below tall trees while hunting. Couple this with the explosion of feral and unwanted cats simply turned loose by uncaring pet owners, and you can see the cottontail has his work cut out for him just to survive his first few months on earth. Other factors have also helped keep the rabbit population from expand-ing: the decline in the sport of trapping (fox, coyotes, and other rabbit predators); the mass destruction of brushy habitat (road building, malls, large housing devel-opments); new and efficient farming methods; and the heavy use of insecticides and defoliants. If the millions of gallons of "green lawn food" sprayed on our yards each year sicken, injure, and even kill humans, what do the chemicals do to a small rabbit eating the stuff? Power companies now routinely aerial spray miles of brushy power line right-of-ways, killing everything beneath the wires. There is no doubt in my mind that this devastating liquid kills rabbits and other animals exposed to it, no matter what the power companies tell us.

Rabbit hunting, although in general decline, will be kept alive by dedicated hunters who simply love the thrill of the chase. Bill Morgan with Annie Oakley.

Adding all these factors together, is it any wonder why rabbit hunting isn't what it once was? In fact, I am surprised sometimes that I find as many rabbits as I do!

On the other side of the coin, organizations such as The American Rabbit Hound Association (ARHA) and Rabbits Unlimited Inc. (RU) have helped to rekindle some of the interest there once was in rabbit hunting. The ARHA was founded by a group of rabbit hunters who had good rabbit gundogs (grade dogs), that were not registered with any other dog organization, so they began "registering" and keeping tract of their dogs' pedigrees. Today, tens of thousands of rabbit dogs are registered with the ARHA, some already going back several generations. The ARHA holds its own wild rabbit trials and awards multiple winners with the title of "Rabbit Champion" or "Grand Rabbit Champion."

Although once owned and published by The American Rabbit Hound Association, The *Rabbit Hunter* magazine has now split off from the dog registry and is headquartered in Royston, Georgia. Trial winners (from several registries), upcoming events, and rabbit hunting stories make up the pages of the magazine. The ARHA has become an excellent medium for rabbit hunters and those searching for old-time rabbit dogs. The *Rabbit Hunter* magazine, along with the American Rabbit Hound Association, are both doing a fine job promoting the sport of rabbit hunting.

Rabbits Unlimited Inc. is a newer organization taking a different approach to rabbit hunting. They want to promote the rabbit much more than the dogs chasing him, which makes sense to me. RU is based in South Carolina. Its goal is to unite rabbit hunters all over the country, raising money for land management, thereby having some influence on rabbit habitat enhancement. In South Carolina, RU has already begun some habitat and research work.

> **The American Rabbit Hound Association**
>
> National Kennel Club
> P.O. Box 331
> Blaine, TN 37709
> 865-932-9680
> www.arha.com
>
> **Rabbits Unlimited**
> P.O. Box 186
> Abbeville, SC 29620
> 864-459-5145
> www.rabbitsunlimited.org
>
> **The Rabbit Hunter Magazine**
> P.O. Box 557
> Royston, GA 30662
> 706-245-0081

Registries and divisions such as the American Kennel Club, United Kennel Club, and American Hunting Basset Association; magazines such as *Small Pack Option*, *Hounds & Hunting*, *The Beagler*, and others; and now even web-sites such as Beagles Unlimited all help to promote and keep the sport of beagling alive.

Despite organizations such as RU, ARHA, and the others listed, I think actual rabbit hunting will slowly continue to decline. Many people simply do not want anyone on their property for any type of hunting these days, and more and more of us are being squeezed onto public hunting areas. Habitat destruction is also a great foe of cottontails and cottontail hunters. Every hunter can tell you about losing a few more treasured spots each year. As mentioned, rabbits are a little tougher to hunt, and good rabbit hunting dogs are increasingly hard to come by. Besides all this, our suburban, hurry-up lifestyle leaves little room for raising dogs or chasing rabbits. Oh, there will always be some dedicated rabbit hunters who can look over the few faults of imperfect hounds, and enjoy the total experience of a cottontail chase.

The cottontail's sheer determination to adapt and survive has kept him alive

Some beaglers have no desire to give up rabbit hunting and some sensational hunting is still available. The author and his friends find the fields and thickets very uncrowded, and plenty of rabbits for the dogs to chase. (left) Larry Russman, the author, Dave Fisher, and Denny Malone (right).

and well in many thickets across the country. He is still listed by most game agencies as the number one game animal in the country. I see this changing little in the years ahead, but I do expect rabbit hunting to experience some further decline, despite a resurgence in the past ten years because of the organizations mentioned. Nothing is more enjoyable for a youngster than an old-fashioned rabbit hunt. But in another respect, these trends are good for rabbit hunters who have no plan or desire to give up rabbit hunting. We find the fields and thickets uncrowded, and it seems there will always be enough rabbits to give the hounds something to do.

The future of rabbit hunting? I have no definitive answers. It is clear that it will certainly be around for quite a few years yet, but I am afraid that real rabbit hunting, the kind that some of us know and love, may be headed for practical extinction. With fewer and fewer places to hunt, fewer and fewer people taking part in it, rabbits under attack from many forces, and fewer and fewer dogs being bred and trained to chase them, things don't look extremely bright for cottontail or hare hunting.

I can only suggest that we enjoy it while it's here, and maybe that in itself can turn things around.

Maybe the future of rabbit hunting will always depend on new hunters coming along. Here Jill Russman is nothing but smiles on her late winter 2001 hunt, her first year hunting.

Rabbit hunting has been part of my life for so long I cannot imagine not doing it. It is the companionship of the dogs, their loyalty, and the camaraderie of a good hunting pal that makes every minute precious.

EPILOGUE

I t has been a struggle to finally get this book finished. Many other oblig-
ations, personal matters, years of work making the videos, and, of course,
the time spent hunting, all have infringed on the time required to complete it. I must certainly thank my wife, Linda, and the others who have
contributed their help in some way. I also thank the friends and fellow
hunters who have appeared in this book, and accompanied me on many rabbit
hunts over the years. There seems to be a special bond that develops between
good hunting companions. I have been privileged to hunt with some great and
unselfish hunters, and continue to meet more as time goes along.

I also could not write a book and not mention some of the great dogs I have
owned or hunted behind. Berries, my first good beagle and loyal friend, how
she is missed, even after all these years. Teddy, how I wish I could turn back the
clock and pick him up again. Buster, Berries' only red son and surely one of the
best hunting dogs I will ever see in my lifetime . . . gone, but never forgotten.
Red Dawn, Sunny, April, Shorty, Red Rover, Hershey, Pontiac, and scores of
others have come and gone; some we rarely think of, others, like Sue-Sue, we
miss until this day. And then there are the dogs that have passed on much more
recently, like Ralphie, Lightning, Annie Oakley, and Bowser; these dogs, when
together, made up one of the finest packs any hunter could ever be privileged
to hunt over. Lightning, sweet Lightning, surely the finest all-round hunting dog
anyone could ever have in his kennel. These dogs were more than just hunting
dogs, but loyal and trusted friends, and literally windows into the past. A new
pack, almost all descendants of Ralphie and Lightning, now takes up residence
in the new barn kennel: Sammy, Storm, Chase, Amber, and Storm's pups Half-
Track-Bruce, 4th of July Boomer, Lightning Bolt, and Stormy Dark Sky.

Rabbit hunting and these dogs have been part of my life for so long that I
can't imagine not having them, or not hunting over them. Oh, there are times
when my body aches and we've been out so long that the entire ordeal begins

to lose the appeal it once had. Then one of the hounds strikes a good track and we forget all about our aching backs and sore tired legs. And after just a few weeks without it, we're anxious for the season to start again.

I have killed a lot of rabbits in my lifetime. I am neither ashamed, nor do I apologize for doing so. Our Lord, in His infinite wisdom, put these animals here for a reason, and it is obvious it wasn't just to eat up the garden. Only in the past quarter century or so, when we have become more "civilized," do we abhor killing, and do it neatly and efficiently in slaughterhouses away from the common eye. It's all killing, and unless we plan to convert the entire planet to vegetarians, it will always be with us.

On the other hand, I have a deep respect and love for this guy I call Mr. Cottontail. He has provided me with countless hours of fun and sheer enjoyment. I protect his nests, try to eliminate the predators constantly striving to take his life, and have nearly wrecked my truck on many occasions trying to avoid him. I'm sure, however, he would survive without any assistance from me.

I hope you have enjoyed this book, going along on many cottontail hunts with me, remembering a few of my greatest runs, and somewhere along the lines picked up some good, useful information. Even as I write this, I can think of several things I neglected to cover, or wanted to, but have simply run out of time and space. A book can never cover everything, but written words on a page seem to come the closest to capturing the spirit of the event without actually being there.

And yet, as I end this book, I find it is still impossible to put into words what rabbit hunting has meant to me. If I was asked the question, "If you had to give up all hunting except one kind, what would it be?" the answer would have to be rabbit hunting. To stand high on an ancient stump in an open woodlot on a January afternoon, a light snow pack melting under a warm overcast sky, a few snowflakes fluttering earthward, listening to the dogs turning my way and knowing Mr. Cottontail is streaking toward me. How could I explain that feeling to anyone who hasn't been there?

As the leaves turn brown and a trickle of snow begins to outline cottontail tracks in some unnamed thicket, I hope to be there, yelling at the dogs and joking with a good hunting buddy. At times like these, nothing on earth seems more important.